Het IJ

S118

Flora Park

NIEUWENDAM

A10

NOORD

SPAARNDAMMERBURT

WH Vliegenbos

SCHELLINGWOUDE

Singelgracht

Centraal Station

IJ-TUNNEL

Het IJ

S114

Anne Frankhuis

Beurs van Berlage

Newmetropolis

IJ Haven

Oosterdok

Dijksgracht

Koninklijk Paleis

CENTRUM

Museum het Rembrandthuis

HAVENS-OOST

Amsterdams Historisch Museum

Stadhuis en Muziektheater

Natura Artis Magistra (Zoo)

IJ Meer

A10

Rijksmuseum

Nederlandse Bank

OOST

Singelgracht

Muiderpoort Station

Flevo-park

Het Nieuwe Diep

Tropenmuseum en Kindermuseum

Oosterpark

OUD ZUID

Sarphatipark

Amstel

Diemer Polder

ZUID

Amstel Kanaal

WATERGRAAFSMEER

A2-E231

BERLAGE-BRUG

Amstel Station

RAI Congrescentrum

eatrixpark

Martin Luther King Park

UTRECHTSE-BRUG

A10

DIEMEN

A10

Amstel-park

OVER AMSTEL

Amstel

DUIVENDRECHT

Duivendrecht

A2-E35

De Rieker

RIJKSWEG

BIJLMERMEER

Amsterdam Arena

Ouderkerker aan-de-Amstel

D

E

F

Amsterdam

Any one of the elements that meld to form Amsterdam's special character would be enough to create a memorable setting. Its thousands of magnificent 17th-century buildings, strung along a web of canals crossed by more than a thousand bridges; its situation below sea-level in a place where, by rights, cold North Sea waves should flow back and forth; the centuries-long tradition of tolerance that made the city a magnet for oppressed minorities long before such a stance became fashionable, or even imaginable, elsewhere; the refusal to settle for what outsiders consider right and proper, but instead to search for their own solutions to all kinds of social challenges, from prostitution, to drug use and abuse; and how to live harmoniously in a melting pot society. The city's often eccentric lifestyle has a downside, and not everybody takes to its free and easy ways. One thing is sure, though: you'll never be bored.

> *'Where else in the world are all life's commodities and every conceivable curiosity to be found as easily as here? Where else in the world can one find such absolute freedom?'*

RENÉ DESCARTES,
Letter to a friend, 1634

---•---

Visit the Albert Cuyp street market for bargains and local colour

The streets are paved with orange on Koninginnedag (Queen's Day)

The City of Amsterdam

This city is easy to get to grips with – geographically speaking. Its centre is small enough for locals to think of it as a village, and many sights and attractions lie within easy walking distance of each other. Once you've learned how to work out which way you're facing on the ring canal network, most of your directional problems are over. Should you grow weary of traipsing cobbled streets you can take the weight off your feet aboard a tram, canal boat, water taxi, even a pedalo (water bike).

The top three museums – Rijksmuseum, Van Gogh Museum and Stedelijk Museum (although the first of these is currently drastically curtailed and the last has moved to temporary premises) – are complemented by a cast of supporting acts covering everything from the city's history, and Holland's glorious maritime past and colonial empire, through theatre and film, to moderately offbeat institutions on such themes as cats and houseboats, and radically offbeat places featuring drugs, torture and sex.

There is much more to Amsterdam, however, than history, museums and art. The city's brown cafés, stained by centuries of tobacco smoke, are much-loved institutions that merit the prized Dutch description '*gezellig*' – comfortable, warm, friendly. Nightlife, drinking and dining options are legion, and if you must, you can take yourself to a 'coffee shop' where you can puff your way through as much officially tolerated hashish as you like.

Amsterdam is an attitude as much as a real place. If you already have, or can acquire, the right attitude, you'll find it's a real place, too.

What to See in Amsterdam

ALLARD PIERSON MUSEUM ✪

Amsterdam University houses its archaeological collection in a neo-classical former bank. There are few outstanding objects, but rather bits and pieces from here and there – coins, funerary monuments, mummies, glassware, jewellery, marble, pottery, sculpture and everyday objects. Pharaonic Egypt, Minoan Crete, ancient Greece, Rome and Etruria are reasonably well represented, and there are some good models of pyramids and chariots. Temporary exhibitions are generally more interesting.

THE AMSTEL ✪✪

Amsterdam's river flows south to north into the city, passing some lovely countryside around Ouderkerk aan de Amstel (► 85) before reaching urban reality as it passes under the A10 ring road. The stretch from Utrechtsebrug to the Blauwbrug (Blue Bridge), lined with houseboats, theatres, cafés and riverside homes, presents a busy

+ 40C3
✉ Oude Turfmarkt 127
☎ 525 2556
🕐 Tue–Fri 10–5, Sat–Sun and pub hols 1–5. Closed 1 Jan, Easter Sun, 30 Apr, 5 May, Whit Sunday 25 Dec
🚊 4, 9, 14, 16, 24, 25
♿ Good
🍴 Moderate

+ 41E1

scene of canal barges, tour boats and private boats travelling up- and downriver. Photographers can't resist the Magere Brug over the Amstel (➤ 57). As it flows past the Muziektheater and Hôtel de l'Europe, the river gradually loses itself among a maze of city-centre canals.

Tour boats show visitors the sights along the Amstel

AMSTELPARK ✪

This beautiful green area, created in 1972 for a decennial national flower show, the Floriade, lies along the River Amstel on the edge of town. It is hemmed in on the north by the busy A10 ring road and on the west by suburban Buitenveldert. You can stroll around its central pond and through a rosarium and rhododendron garden, get lost in a maze, and visit the Glazenhuis (Glass House) art gallery and a children's farm. De Rieker windmill is just outside the park to the south (➤ 67).

- 🔲 29D1
- ✉ Between Amsteldijk and Europaboulevard
- 🕐 Park: dawn–dusk; Glazenhuis: Mar–Nov Mon–Fri 10–5
- 🍴 Rosarium café-restaurant (€–€€)
- 🚌 Bus 69, 89, 148, 169
- ♿ Very good
- 🎫 Free

AMSTERDAMSE BOS ✪✪✪

It looks natural, but Amsterdam Wood is man-made. Amsterdammers come to this 900-hectare forested park on the city's southern edge for fresh air and to escape from the city. Many bring a picnic when the weather is fine. With its trees and plants firmly established in what was once open polder, the park is home to birds, insects and small animals, and its lakes and wetland zones attract water birds. Trace its history and learn about the plants and wildlife at the new Bezoekerscentrum (Visitors Centre).

The list of open-air activities is lengthy. In addition to a bicycle-hire kiosk beside the main entrance, there are stables where you can hire horses and tour the park on bridle-paths, sport facilities, children's play areas, picnic tables, an open-air theatre, a goat farm, boating, rowing competitions on the 2km-long Roeibaan lake, and more.

In summer, take a tram ride on an antique car from the Trammuseum at Haarlemmermeerstation (➤ 72), and on Sundays and holidays, in good weather, a little ferryboat makes trips across the Nieuwe Meer (New Lake).

- 🔲 28B1
- ✉ Main entrance: Amstelveenseweg. Visitors Centre: Bosbaanweg 5
- ☎ Visitors Centre: 545 6100
- 🕐 Park: always open; Visitors Centre: daily 12–5
- 🍴 De Bosbaan café, De Manegerie café (€–€€)
- 🚌 Bus 170, 171, 172
- ♿ Very good
- 🎫 Free

Along the Amstel

Cycling is a key ingredient in the Amsterdam experience and on this riverside route you get a breath of fresh country air as a bonus. Pause at the start for a look at the Blauwbrug (Blue Bridge).

Carré: theatrical highlight down by the riverside

Facing south (upriver), cycle along the Amstel's east or right bank (the river should be on your right), across Nieuwe Herengracht and Nieuwe Keizersgracht to the Magere Brug (➤ 57). Cross Nieuwe Prinsengracht to a set of locks beside which stands the Koninklijke Theater Carré (➤ 112). Continue over Sarphatistraat to the Amstel InterContinental Hotel.

The city's top hotel, the Amstel is favoured by blue bloods, Hollywood superstars and top musicians.

Dogleg around behind the hotel, back to the river on Weesperzijde, and past De IJsbreker contemporary music centre. Continue to the Berlagebrug, where you cross to the left bank.

The bridge, which has red-and-black painted lampposts, was built in 1932 by Hendrik Petrus Berlage, designer of the Beurs van Berlage (➤ 38), and a forerunner of the Amsterdam School of Architecture.

Continue south, past Martin Luther Kingpark and houseboats moored along Amsteldijk, to Amstelpark (➤ 33), the De Rieker windmill (➤ 67) and a statue of Rembrandt.

You are now in open countryside, passing through idyllic riverside scenery on the way to Ouderkerk aan de Amstel (➤ 85). Explore the pretty, historic village.

For the return to Amsterdam, take Ouderkerkerdijk on the right bank of the river.

You pass through several hamlets on this tranquil road.

Keep going to busy Utrechtsebrug. Cross over to Amsteldijk and stay on the left bank all the way back to the Blue Bridge.

Distance
20km

Time
4–6 hours

Start/end point
Blauwbrug
✚ 41D2
🚇 Waterlooplein
🚊 9, 14
🚢 Museum Boat stop 3

Lunch
't Klein Kalfje (€, ➤ 94)

Bike hire
MacBike
✉ Mr Visserplein 2
☎ 620 0985

AMSTERDAMS HISTORISCH MUSEUM (▶ 16, TOP TEN)

AMSTERDAMS VERZETSMUSEUM ✪

The Resistance Museum tells the story of Amsterdam's five years (1940–5) under Nazi occupation during World War II. Among the events it highlights are the 1941 February Strike against the deportation of the city's Jewish population, and the terrible 'Hunger Winter' of 1944–5, as well as the minutiae of underground activities: illegal newspapers, espionage, sabotage, assassination.

ANNE FRANKHUIS (▶ 17, TOP TEN)

ARTIS ✪✪✪

Holland's largest zoo houses more than 6,000 animals, including lions, tigers, leopards, elephants and rhinoceroses. Its full name is Natura Artis Magistra: 'Nature, Teacher of the Arts', and among its attractions are extensive gardens whose range of tree and plant varieties almost rivals that of nearby Hortus Botanicus (▶ 49). Artis does its best to replicate the animals' natural environment, using glass and perspex to get you close to them. Good examples are the Reptile House, with its steamy jungle settings, and the renovated 1882 Aquarium, which has glass tanks in which seals disport, as well as displays on coral reefs, the Amazon and a surprising, cut-away view of an Amsterdam canal, with fish swimming beside a sunken bicycle and other urban detritus. To get value from the steep admission price, visit, at no extra charge, the excellent Planetarium, Geological Museum and Zoological Museum. If you have young children don't let them miss the children's farm.

✚ 41E3
✉ Plantage Kerklaan 61a
☎ 620 2535
🕐 Tue–Fri 10–5, Sat–Mon & public hols 12–5. Closed 1 Jan, 30 Apr, 25 Dec
🚍 6
♿ Good
💵 Cheap

✚ 41E2
✉ Plantage Kerklaan 38–40
☎ 523 3400
🕐 Daily 9–5 (to 6 Apr–Oct); Planetarium closed Mon morning
🍴 Artis restaurant (€)
🚍 6, 9, 14
🚢 Artis Express boat from Centraal Station
♿ Good
💵 Very expensive

Above: *Artis has a way with animals, and a leafy, garden-like setting*

35

In the Know

If you only have a short time to visit Amsterdam and would like to get a real flavour of the city, here are some ideas:

10
Ways to be a Local

Go Dutch. Almost everyone speaks English, but an occasional *Alstublieft* (please) and *Dank u wel* (thank you) can go a long way.

Don't walk in bicycle lanes. And don't complain if a cyclist thumps you because you did.

Don't be seen dead on a water bike – by all means be seen alive on one,

Waterborne revellers celebrate Queen's Day (30 April)

though, for a great experience that many locals pass up.

Take flowers (tulips are OK) if someone invites you

Settling into Café 't Smalle's welcoming ambience

to their home for dinner.

Head for a café terrace at the first hint of sunshine.

Eat raw herring at a street stall.

Wear something orange on Koninginnedag, Queen Beatrix's official birthday (30 April).

Don't criticise Holland, the Dutch way of doing things or the Queen; it's OK to make jibes about other members of the royal family.

Get the time right. If you have an appointment at 30 minutes past the hour, half ten say, make sure it's not *half tien*, which means 9:30, not 10:30.

Absorb the atmosphere in a 'coffee shop'. Relatively few Amsterdammers are among those who smoke joints in these places; tourists are a big part of the clientele.

Join the crowds in search of a bargain, or just browsing, at the Albert Cuyp street market

10
Top Places to Have Lunch

Café Américain (➤ 93)
Café Roux (➤ 93)
De Jaren (➤ 94)
Excelsior (€€€)
✉ Hôtel de l'Europe, Nieuwe Doelenstraat 2–8 ☎ 531 1777. Formal elegance and top-flight continental cuisine.
't Klein Kalfje (➤ 94)
De Kas (➤ 94)
Luxembourg (➤ 95)
Pancake Bakery (€)
✉ Prinsengracht 191 ☎ 625 1333. Traditional and wildly inventive pancakes.
Royal Café De Kroon (➤ 96)
Vertigo (➤ 97)

10
Top Activities

Pass an hour in the 'company' of Anne Frank, in the secret refuge where she wrote her famous diary (➤ 17).
Visit Zandvoort on Sunday, whatever the weather, and walk up and down along the beach (➤ 89).
Hire a bicycle (➤ 34) and dice with the trams at Leidseplein.
Spend an evening in a traditional Amsterdam brown café (➤ this page and ➤ 114).
Take a tour by canal boat; it's the best way to get a quick overview of the city (➤ 67).
Hear the Royal Concertgebouw Orchestra at the Concertgebouw (➤ 44).
Applaud Amsterdam's ace football team Ajax at Amsterdam ArenA (➤ 115).
Spend a few hours at the Albert Cuypmarkt and the Waterlooplein flea market, or wander around one of the other markets listed (➤ 106).

Eat your way through the 10–20 little dishes of a *rijsttafel*, an Indonesian speciality (created by the Dutch).
Beg, borrow, steal, or even buy ice-skates if the canals freeze (➤ 115).

5
Best Views From

• Herengracht bridge at Thorbeckeplein (➤ 47).
• IJ Ferry (➤ 50).
• Magere Brug (➤ 57).
• Westertoren (➤ 26).
• Zuidertoren (➤ 75).

10
Best Brown Cafés

➤ 114
• De Druif
• De Engelbewaarder
• Hoppe
• De Karpershoek
• 't Loosje
• Papeneiland
• De Reiger
• Reijnders
• 't Smalle
• Tabac

Roam the city on a bike – the locals do

37

DID YOU KNOW?

In 1555 the Habsburg Emperor Charles V turned over the Low Countries to his son, the future King Philip II of Spain. Philip, an ardent Catholic, set about oppressing Protestantism. Amsterdam remained neutral in the struggle that broke out until 1578, when its Calvinist merchants overthrew the city's Catholic council in an event remembered as the *Alteratie* (Alteration) and threw in their lot with the Dutch rebellion led by William of Orange against the Spanish .

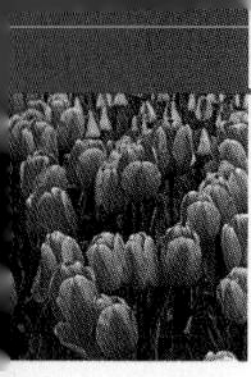

ATHENAEUM ILLUSTRE

A Renaissance gateway from 1571 marks the entrance to Amsterdam's first university. Founded in 1631, it took over the 15th-century Gothic Agnietenkapel (St Agnes Chapel) and Franciscan convent, which was used as an arsenal by the Dutch navy after the 1578 religious *Alteratie*. It now houses the Universiteitsmuseum (University Museum), embracing the university's history, professors and students.

- 40C3
- Oudezijds Voorburgwal 231
- 525 3339
- Mon–Fri 9–5, Sun (late Jun to mid-Nov) 2–5. Closed pub hols
- 4, 9, 14, 16, 24, 25
- Free (except special exhibitions)

BEGIJNHOF (► 18, TOP TEN)

BEURS VAN BERLAGE

Hendrik Petrus Berlage's 1903, red-brick Beurs (Stock Exchange) is an early work of the Amsterdam School, whose members made a dramatic break with 19th-century architecture. No longer the stock exchange, it hosts concerts and exhibitions, and its south wing is home to the Beurs van Berlage Museum, with displays on the Stock Exchange's history and temporary exhibitions on varying themes. The interior has interesting glass and wrought-iron decoration and murals. Among exterior sculptures, a relief of two fishermen and a sick dog in a boat illustrates a legend of the city's foundation (► 44). Climb the clock tower for a view of the old centre. Trees and 19th-century wrought-iron street lamps dot neighbouring Beursplein.

- 41D4
- Damrak 277
- 624 0141
- Tue–Sun 11–5
- Café Rainieri (€)
- 4, 9, 14, 16, 24, 25
- Good
- Moderate

BIJBELS MUSEUM

The Biblical Museum's twin canal houses, with richly decorated neck-gables and a courtyard with an ornamental garden, are worth visiting for their intrinsic interest. They were built in 1662 by architect Philips Vingboons for wealthy merchant Jacob Cromhout. In 1717, Jacob de Wit painted the main hall's ceiling with classical scenes. The collection focuses on life in the Holy Land during biblical times and on Judaism and Christianity through the centuries. Objects on view include a model of ancient Jerusalem, models of the temples of Solomon and Herod, one of them dating from 1730, a model of the Tabernacle

- 40B3
- Herengracht 366–368
- 624 2436
- Mon–Sat 10–5, Sun and pub hols 1–5. Closed 1 Jan, 30 Apr
- 1, 2, 5
- Museum Boat stop 4
- None
- Moderate

from 1851, and archaeological finds and paintings of biblical scenes. Bibles include the first one printed in the Low Countries, in 1477, and a first edition of the authorised Dutch translation from 1637.

BIJLMERMEER ✪

Until recent years, this district in the southeast of the city was fast becoming a ghetto with crime and drug addiction rife. It reached rock bottom in 1992 when an Israeli El Al cargo aircraft crashed into a tower block, killing 43 people. Since then money has been invested to redevelop the area. This process has been aided by the opening of Ajax football club's giant Amsterdam ArenA stadium, and the Amsterdam Poort shopping, commercial and entertainment complex. The 'Bijlmer', as the district is known locally has come up a little in the world. It's still no paradise but it adds a wider social context to a visit to this city.

BLOEMENMARKT ✪✪

Like an Impressionist artist's palette fallen from the sky the Singel Flower Market, Amsterdam's only remaining floating market (though it no longer floats, exactly), is a riot of colour. A floating market was established here in the 17th century; now a row of 15 shops partially installed on permanently moored barges sell bunches of freshly cut flowers as fast as the sales staff can wrap them, along with plants, packets of tulip bulbs with phytosanitary certificates that permit their import into many countries, and all kinds of green-fingered accessories. Buying flowers along the fragrantly scented canalside is an Amsterdam ritual, though prices are no cheaper than those in shops.

➕ 28F1

Above: there's no better place to buy flowers than the floating Flower Market

➕ 40C2
✉ Singel (between Muntplein and Koningsplein)
🕐 Mon–Sat 9:30–5:30 (till 5 Sat).
🚊 1, 2, 4, 5, 9, 14, 16,24, 25
⛴ Museum Boat stop 4
♿ Good
 Free

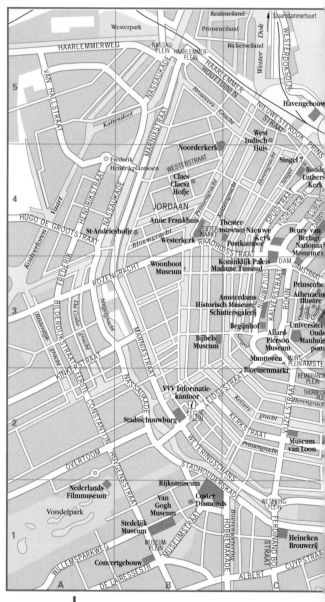

CENTRAL AMSTERDAM

Het IJ

BUIKSLOTERWEG

Noord Hollandsch Kanaal

MEEUWENLAAN

IJ-TUNNEL

DE RUIJTERKADE

KNSM Eiland

ntraal
Station

ATIONS 🅼 Centraal Station
PLEIN

IJ-Haven

ℹ️

PIET HEINKADE

& KADE St Nicolaaskerk
ure
scums   Schreierstoren

Dijksgracht

Museum Amstelkring

Scheepvaarthuis

de   Erotisch
rl   Museum   Newmetropolis
            Waag
Tattoo   NIEUWMARKT
Museum
Has   Nieuw-   🅼
Marihuana   Markt   Montelbaan-
Hemp Museum   storen
Oostindisch Huis   Nederlands
   Trippenhuis   Scheepvaart Museum
   Zuiderkerk

Holland   Museum het   Amsterdams
xperience   Rembrandthuis   Verzetsmuseum
   Stadhuis en   MR VISSER Mozes en Aäronkerk
   Muziektheater   PLEIN   Wertheim   Werf 't
                   Park   Kromhout
   Portugese
   Synagoge   Planetarium   De Gooier
Waterlooplein 🅼   Hortus
STELSTR BLAUW Joods Botanicus Hollandse   Natura Artis
      BRUG   Historisch Plantage Schouwburg   Magistra
Museum   Museum   (Zoo)   Zoölogisch
Willet-   Museum-
Holthuysen   Nieuwe   MIDDENLAAN   Aquarium

MAGERE
BRUG   Nieuwe

   Koninklijke   Weesper-   🅼   Tropenmuseum
   Theater   plein   en Kindermuseum
   Carré
                        Oosterpark
FREDERIKS-
PLEIN
   Nederlandse
   Bank   De Ijsbreker   Gasthuis
STADHOUDERSKADE
                        OOSTERPARKSTRAAT

rphatipark CEINTURBAAN

   Amstel   Wibautstraat 🅼

0   200   400 m

D   E   F

Converted 17th-century warehouses mirrored in the Brouwersgracht

🚇 40B5
✉ Between Lijnbaansgracht and Singel
🍴 De Belhamel (▶ 92); Café Tabac, Brouwersgracht 101 (€)
🚋 1, 2, 5, 6, 13, 17

BROUWERSGRACHT ⭐⭐

The 'Brewers' Canal' owes its name to its 16th- and 17th-century brewery *pakhuizen* (warehouses), many now chic apartments. Attractively restored, De Kroon (The Crown) at No 118, and the modern Blauwe Burgt apartment block show how old and new are trying to live in harmony. The point where Brouwersgracht joins Prinsengracht is one of the most photogenic spots in the city. At Herenmarkt, off Brouwersgracht, is West-Indisch Huis (West India House), which in 1623 became the Dutch West India Company's headquarters. In its courtyard is a bronze statue of Peter Stuyvesant, governor of Nieuw Amsterdam from 1646 until 1664, when the British took over and renamed it New York. A sculpture depicts the first Dutch settlement on Manhattan Island, founded in 1624.

✉ Rijksmuseum, Leidseplein, Keizersgracht/Leidsestraat (rarely open), Anne Frankhuis
☎ 626 5574
🕐 Apr–Jun and Sep–Oct daily 10–7; Jul–Aug daily 10–10 (may close earlier)
♿ None
💶 Expensive

CANAL BIKE ⭐⭐

Amsterdammers scorn them, but it's hard to think of a better way of touring the city's canals, short of having your own boat. On these two- and four-seat pedalos (water bikes) you can view the canals and their gabled houses at your own pace and from a unique perspective. You can hire a pedalo at one of four Canal Bike moorings near popular sights around the centre and leave it at another. The company provides maps and basic 'rules of the road'.

🚇 41D4
✉ Stationsplein
🍴 1e Klas (€–€€), Smits Koffiehuis (€)
🚋 1, 2, 4, 5, 6, 9, 13, 16, 17, 24, 25
🚢 Museum Boat stop 1
♿ Excellent

CENTRAAL STATION ⭐⭐

Amsterdam's main railway station is a bustling hub that captures the city's energy, bundles it up and sends it hurrying off again in all directions. Eleven of 16 tram lines converge here, along with four metro lines, passenger ferries, any number of buses, canal buses, taxis, water-taxis and tour boats (including the Museumboat and the Canal Bus). There are two VVV (Vereniging voor

Amsterdam's Centraal Station is much more than a transport hub

Vreemdelingenverkeer) city tourist offices, one inside on platform two, the other outside on Stationsplein; a Grenswisselkantoor (GWK) exchange office; cafés; shops; buskers; barrel-organs; a million bicycles, commuters, tourists, backpackers, pickpockets and junkies.

Petrus Josephus Hubertus Cuypers designed this work of architectural note, which opened in 1889 on three artificial islands in the IJ channel. Cuypers, who also designed the Rijksmuseum (➤ 22–3), repeated his earlier trick of mixing Dutch Renaissance elements with his own neo-gothic inclinations, to produce a twin-towered temple of transport that, at the time, many Amsterdammers were inclined to hate.

CLAES CLAESZOON HOFJE ⭐

Wealthy cloth merchant Claes Claeszoon Anslo founded this almshouse in 1615. It is really two *hofjes*, whose tiny houses surrounding two picturesque little courtyards are now music students' homes. You can visit the courtyards when the outer door is open.

🚇 40B4
✉️ Egelantiersstraat 18–50/ Eerste Egelantiersdwars-straat 1–3
🚊 6, 13, 14, 17
♿ Free

COBRA MUSEUM ⭐⭐

Begun in 1948, the Cobra group took its name from the founding artists' home cities: Copenhagen, Brussels and Amsterdam. In creating a new, post-war art, they reached for childlike, spontaneous imagery, often done in bold colours with crayon, that laid the foundations of abstract expressionism. Their first exhibition, at Amsterdam's Stedelijk Museum (➤ 71) in 1949, ignited fierce controversy. Cobra has since become more accepted and now has this permanent home. Vividly expressionistic works by Karel Appel, Asger Jorn and Pierre Alechinsky are among those on display at the dazzlingly white museum in respectable, suburban Amstelveen.

🚇 28C1
✉️ Sandbergplein 1–3, Amstelveen
☎️ 547 5050
🕐 Tue–Sun 11–5. Closed 1 Jan, 1 Apr, 30 Apr, 25 Dec
🍴 Café-restaurant (€)
🚊 51 Amstelveen
🚌 5
♿ Excellent
💶 Moderate

43

Concertgebouw strikes just the right notes for classical music

🕂 40B1
✉ Concertgebouwplein 2–6
☎ 671 8345
🕐 Box office daily 10–7;
8:15 for tickets same day
🍴 Café (€)
🚌 3, 5, 12, 16 ♿ Good
⚘ Lunchtime concerts free;
otherwise moderate to
expensive
❓ Guided tours by prior
arrangement Sun 9:30

🕂 40B1
✉ Paulus Potterstraat 2–6
☎ 305 5555
🕐 Daily 9–5. Closed 25 Dec
🚌 2, 5
🚢 Museum Boat stop 6
♿ Few
⚘ Free

🕂 40C3
🚌 1, 2, 4, 6, 5, 9, 13, 14, 16,
17, 24, 25

CONCERTGEBOUW

Classical musicians consider the home of the Koninklijke Concertgebouworkest (Royal Concertgebouw Orchestra), which opened in 1888, to be one of the world's most accoustically perfect concert halls. Architect Adolf van Gendt designed it in neo-Dutch renaissance style with a neo-classical colonnade. Portrait busts of Beethoven, Sweelinck and Bach greet you at the entrance, and a sculpted lyre adorns the roof. There are two performance halls, the Grote Zaal (Grand Hall) and the Kleine Zaal (Little Hall), which is used for recitals.

COSTER DIAMONDS

This is one of the several quality diamond workshops in the city to offer guided tours. Amsterdam got into the diamond business around 1586, when diamond-workers and traders from Bruges and Antwerp, many of whom were Jewish, fled to the city to escape the Spanish Inquisition. Such famous diamonds as the Cullinan and Koh-I-Noor were cut in Amsterdam. Coster's 30-minute tour includes a brief history of diamonds, and it is fascinating to watch the company's craftspeople at work, cutting, polishing, sorting and setting.

DAM

Foreigners say 'Dam Square', but to Amsterdammers it's 'the Dam', though it is evidently a square and not a dam. The original dam, built in the early-13th century, protected

---

DID YOU KNOW?

A shaggy dog story competes with the historical record of Amsterdam's foundation. Two fishermen and a dog, their boat caught in a Zuiderzee storm, made landfall at what is now Zeedijk. The dog jumped on to dry land and promptly threw up, thereby marking the spot. An image of two men and a seasick dog in a boat appears on the city's old coat of arms, which you can see at various places around town.

what was then a fishing village. As Amsterdam expanded, flood defences were built further away and the Dam developed into the political, commercial, monumental and ceremonial heart of the city, containing the Royal Palace (► 19), Nieuwe Kerk (► 62) and Nationaal Monument (► 60). It frequently hosts fairs, concerts and other events.

DE EILANDEN (THE ISLANDS)

Along the IJ waterfront's southern shore, redevelopment is transforming artificial islands that once held harbour installations, boat repair yards and warehouses. On the Western Islands of Prinseneiland, Bickerseiland and Realeneiland, northwest of Centraal Station, old warehouses are now desirable apartments. On KNSM Eiland, east of Centraal Station, modern apartments replace cargo-handling facilities.

EROTISCH MUSEUM

'The Art of Erotics' is how the owners subtitle their establishment. Prints and drawings, including some by John Lennon, and photographs aim to uncover the artistic side of eroticism and sado-masochism. Attractions include a maquette of a Red Light District scene and an adult cartoon version of *Snow White and the Seven Dwarfs*.

DE GOOIER (FUNENMOLEN)

Built in 1725 on a brick base with octagonal body and thatched wooden frame, one of the few surviving city windmills houses Brouwerij 't IJ, a small brewery and *proeflokaal* (► 114). It occasionally whirls into action.

➕ 40B5
✉ IJ waterfront
🚌 3; bus 18, 22, 32, 35, 39, 59

Above: *anything can happen, and often does, on the city's monumental square – the Dam*

➕ 41D4
✉ Oudezijds Achterburgwal 54
☎ 624 7303
🕐 Mon–Thu, Sun 11AM–1AM; Fri–Sat 11AM–2AM
🚌 4, 9, 14, 16, 24, 25
♿ Few 🎫 Cheap

➕ 41F2
✉ Funenkade 7
☎ 622 8325
🕐 Wed–Sun 3–8 🚌 7, 10
♿ Good 🎫 Free

45

40C4
✉ Oudezijds Achterburgwal 130
☎ 623 5961 ⏰ Daily 11–10
🚌 4, 9, 14, 16, 24, 25
♿ Few 🍴 Expensive

40C1
✉ Stadhouderskade 78
☎ 523 9666
⏰ Tue–Sun 10–6. Closed 1 Jan, 25 Dec
🍴 Heineken Bar
🚌 16, 24, 25
♿ Few (call ahead)
🍴 Expensive
❓ Over 18s only

Below: *beer on the hoof from Heineken's promotion team*

40C4
🍴 Bars, cafés and restaurants (€–€€€)
🚌 1, 2, 4, 5, 6, 9, 13, 14, 16, 17, 24, 25
🚢 Museum Boat stop 4, 7

HASH MARIHUANA HEMP MUSEUM

An 'educational' tour informs you of the good things that ostensibly flow from smoking and otherwise assimilating hemp's multifarious, stimulating by-products. You will see displays on historical, medicinal, religious, recreational and practical uses of hashish and marijuana.

HEINEKEN EXPERIENCE AMSTERDAM

The old Heineken brewery from 1868 hung up its mash-staff in 1988 and reopened two years later as a museum. The sedate old exhibition has given way to a high-tech, high-energy, multimedia, hands-on series of interactions

> ### DID YOU KNOW?
>
> Contrary to popular opinion, drugs are not legal in Holland. Penalties for possessing and selling heroin, cocaine and other 'hard' drugs are heavy. 'Soft' drugs, such as hashish and marijuana, are also illegal, but Amsterdam's authorities tolerate their sale in small quantities in licensed 'coffee shops'. You are allowed to possess up to 30g of these drugs for personal use, though coffee shops can sell you only 5g at a time.

that all but rams the Heineken marketing message down visitors' throats. Fortunately the experience is otherwise entertaining and there's a glass or two to enjoy at the end.

HERENGRACHT

No fewer than 400 buildings along this historic 2.3km canal are protected monuments. Just as self-made gentlemen were more highly regarded in 17th-century Holland than emperors and princes, so the Gentlemen's Canal, begun in 1609, was a better address than the contemporaneous

Keizersgracht and Prinsengracht. The higher you progress in house numbers, the more ostentatious become the mansions, until you reach the apex of social exclusivity, the Golden Bend, between Leidsestraat and Vijzelstraat.

Highlights of Herengracht's horseshoe-shaped course through the city are its oldest warehouses at Nos 43–5, from around 1600; Theatermuseum at Nos 168–72 (➤ 72); Bijbels Museum at Nos 366–8 (➤ 39); matching neck-gabled houses, the 'twin sisters', at Nos 390–2 and 'twin brothers' at Nos 409–11; the Jewel of Canal Houses at No 475; Kattenkabinet (Cat Cabinet) at No 497; the mayoral residence at No 502; and Museum Willet-Holthuysen at No 605 (➤ 59).

Above: *elegant merchants' houses line Herengracht's prestigious banks*

HERMITAGE AMSTERDAM ✪✪
Opened in 2004 in the rambling 17th-century Amstelhof building and annexes on the east bank of the River Amstel, this Amsterdam offshoot of St Petersburg's State Hermitage Museum won't be completed until 2007. The first phase sets the scene with a changing series of exhibitions of elements from the Russian museum's vast collection of art, fine art and crafts.

➕ 41D2
✉ Neerlandia Gebouw (Building), Nieuwe Herengracht 14
☎ 530 8755
🕐 Daily 10–5
Ⓜ Waterlooplein 🚌 9, 14
🚢 Museum Boat stop 5
♿ Good 💷 Moderate

HOLLAND EXPERIENCE ✪✪
Sit in an aeroplane seat, strap yourself in, metaphorically speaking, and head off on a tour of Holland's landscapes and attractions, by way of a multidimensional film show accompanied by movement, sights, sounds and smells, and for which you have to wear 3-D glasses. Tulip fields, skating on frozen canals, Rembrandt's *The Night Watch*, Queen Beatrix – it's all here.

➕ 41D3
✉ Waterlooplein 17
☎ 422 2233
🕐 Daily 10–6 (shows throughout the day)
Ⓜ Waterlooplein 🚌 9, 14
🚢 Museum Boat stop 3
♿ Very good 💷 Expensive

The Canal Ring

This stroll along the *grachtengordel* takes you through the heart of Golden Age Amsterdam.

From its junction with the Amstel, walk along Herengracht, keeping the canal on your left-hand side, to Museum Willet-Holthuysen (► 59) then to Thorbeckeplein. Cross the canal and go south along Reguliersgracht to Keizersgracht. Turn right along the canal to Museum Van Loon (► 59).

Tour the museum, one of the city's finest canal houses.

Turn right on Vijzelstraat then left on Herengracht.

The next canal bend is the famous Golden Bend, where the city's richest 17th-century citizens had their homes.

Keep going along Herengracht, across Leidse-straat, to the Bijbels Museum (► 39). Turn left on Huidenstraat and right on Keizersgracht.

Note the neo-classical Felix Meritis (Happiness from Merit) building dating from 1787 at No 324, former headquarters of a Calvinist scientific and philosophical society.

Keep going on Keizersgracht, turn left on Reestraat, and right on Prinsengracht. Cross Raadhuisstraat to Westermarkt.

Visit the Westerkerk (► 26) and see the Homomonument, a pink granite monument dedicated to all gay and lesbian people persecuted for their sexual orientation, and a statue of Anne Frank. Visit the Anne Frankhuis (► 17).

Turn right on Leliegracht, and right on Herengracht to the Theatermuseum (► 72). Turn around and go north on Herengracht, turn left on Herenstraat, cross Keizersgracht, and right on Prinsengracht to Noordermarkt.

Visit the Noorderkerk (► 63).

Take Prinsengracht to Brouwersgracht.

Golden Age houses along Herengracht

Distance
4km

Time
2 hours, longer if you visit museums, churches and markets along the way

Start point
Southern end of Herengracht at junction with the River Amstel
✚ 40C2
🚇 Waterlooplein
🚊 4, 9, 14
🚤 Museum Boat stop 5

End point
Brouwersgracht
✚ 40B5
🚇 Centraal Station
🚊 1, 2, 4, 5, 6, 9, 13, 16, 17, 24, 25 (from Centraal Station)
🚤 Museum Boat stop 1

Lunch
Het Land van Walem (► 94)
Luxembourg (► 95)

HOLLANDSCHE SCHOUWBURG ⊗

Only the ruined façade remains of this operetta theatre from 1892, which in 1941 became the Jewish-only Joodsche Schouwburg, an assembly point for Dutch Jews awaiting deportation to concentration camps. It is now a memorial to those 'who ... did not return', with a list of deportees' family names, an eternal flame and a small museum showing items belonging to some of the 60,000 people the Nazis herded here on their way to death.

➕ 41E2
✉ Plantage Middenlaan 24
☎ 626 9945
🕐 Daily 11–4
🚌 6, 9, 14
♿ Very good
✋ Free

HORTUS BOTANICUS ⊗⊗

With 250,000 flowers and 115,000 plants and trees from more than 8,000 varieties, including rare and endangered species, the city's botanical garden has one of the world's largest collections. Founded in 1638 as the Hortus Medicus, for growing medicinal plants and herbs from the Dutch East and West Indies, Australia, South Africa and Japan, Holland's second oldest such garden, after Leiden's (1587), moved here in 1682. At the turn of the century it expanded as a botanical research centre attached to Amsterdam University, and in 1987, when this role ended, went independent and has flourished ever since. This colourful, scented oasis is a great place to escape the crowds. Highlights include the Semicircle, a replica of part of its 1682 layout; the Tri-Climate House, opened in 1993, that brings together African, South American and Mediterranean plants; the Palm House, with 300-year-old palm trees that are among the world's oldest; and the Mexico/California Desert House.

➕ 41D2
✉ Plantage Middenlaan 2a
☎ 625 9021
🕐 Feb–Nov Mon–Fri 9–5, Sat–Sun 11–5; Dec–Jan Mon–Fri 9–4, Sat–Sun 10–4. Closed 1 Jan, 25 Dec
🍴 De Oranjerie (€)
🚌 9, 14
♿ Very good
✋ Moderate

Above: *rainforest below sea level at Hortus Botanicus*

 41D5

Centraal Station

1, 2, 4, 5, 6, 9, 13, 16, 17, 24, 25

Museum Boat stop 1

Historic Ferry cruises leave at 12, 2 and 4; lasts two hours

Above: *passing through the Sint-Antoniessluis in the Jewish Quarter*

HET IJ

The IJ (pronounced like 'eye' in English), an inlet of the IJsselmeer lake, was once the city's harbour. In the 17th century, warehouses filled with exotic products brought from all over the world lined the waterfront. Although large cargo ships now use newer facilities west of the city, beside the North Sea Canal, the IJ remains busy with canal barges, pleasure craft, tour boats and an occasional warship and cruise liner. Free passenger-and-bicycle ferries shuttle back and forth across the channel between the rear of Centraal Station and Amsterdam-Noord, affording a fine view of the harbour during their brief crossings. On Sundays and public holidays (excluding Koninginnedag, 30 April) from Easter until mid-October, a Historic Ferry tour leaves from the dock behind Centraal Station for cruises around the old harbour installations in the eastern IJ.

For an insight into the IJ's colourful maritime past, visit the Nederlands Scheepvaartmuseum (➤ 60) and the redeveloped Western and Eastern Islands, on either side of Centraal Station.

JODENHOEK

Jewish refugees escaping persecution in Europe began arriving in Amsterdam in the 16th century, settling on cheap, marshy land between Nieuwmarkt and the Amstel, around what is now Waterlooplein and Jodenbreestraat. Little remains of the once thriving Jewish Quarter, which,

41D3

Waterlooplein, Nieuwmarkt

9, 14

Museum Boat stop 3

until World War II, never descended to the status of a ghetto. Of the city's 60,000-strong pre-war Jewish population, only about 6,000 survived the Holocaust. During the 1944–5 Hunger Winter, Amsterdammers stripped wood from the quarter's empty buildings to burn as fuel and many unsafe houses were demolished after the war, with more falling victim to redevelopment. Remnants and echoes include the Joods Historisch Museum (see below), the Hollandsche Schouwburg (► 49), the 1675 Portugees-Israëlietische Synagoge (► 65), Waterlooplein Flea Market (► 106), and a Waterlooplein monument to Jewish Resistance fighters.

A silver menorah inside the Jewish Historical Museum

JOODS HISTORISCH MUSEUM ●●●

The remarkable Jewish Historical Museum, occupying four former synagogues in the heart of the Jewish Quarter (see above), records four centuries of Jewish history, identity, religion and culture in the Netherlands. Glassed-in walkways connect the Ashkenazi Synagogue (1670) to the Obbene (1686), Dritt (1700) and New (1752) synagogues. Located here since 1987, the museum puts on temporary exhibitions on international Jewish themes in addition to displaying its permanent collection, which includes historical paintings, decorations, religious and ceremonial objects, clothing, a section on the Holocaust and contemporary Jewish art.

In the square behind the museum is a sculpture called *The Dockworker*, commemorating the February 1941 general strike, led by the city's dockworkers, against Nazi deportation of the Jewish population.

✚ 41D2
✉ Jonas Daniël Meijerplein 2–4
☎ 626 9945
🕐 Daily 11–5. Closed Yom Kippur
🍴 Kosher café (€)
Ⓜ Waterlooplein
🚊 9, 14
🚢 Museum Boat stop 5
♿ Very good
Ⓜ Moderate

DID YOU KNOW?

In what must have been music to Jewish ears, the great Dutch jurist and humanist Hugo Grotius (1583–1645), in his *Remonstratie* (1614), welcomed Jewish refugees who had fled to Holland to escape persecution: 'Plainly God desires them to live somewhere. Why not here rather than elsewhere? The scholars among them may even be of service to us by teaching us the Hebrew language.'

Food & Drink

Gone are the days when Amsterdam was known for its stodgy, unimaginative Dutch food. The scene has been transformed by an influx of cuisine styles from around the world.

Above: *Dutch bakers sell a range of tasty* koeken *(cakes)*
Below: *Gouda cheese*

Borrelhapjes
For taking the edge off your *jenever* and *pils*, two popular 'drink snacks' are *bitterballen* (bitter balls), deep-fried balls of vegetable paste; and *vlammetjes* (little flames), mini spring rolls filled with meat and *sambal*, a hot Indonesian spice.

Breakfast
A Dutch breakfast (*ontbijt*) usually comprises coffee, tea or hot chocolate, a boiled egg, slices of cheese, ham and salami, bread, gingerbread, butter and jam.

Lunch
You can eat a dinner-type meal in a restaurant, but Amsterdammers prefer a light lunch, often bought from a neighbourhood fish stall. This could be *maatjes* (▶ Seafood) or *lekkerbek* (fried fish). In an *eetcafé* (bar-restaurant), a traditional favourite is *uitsmijter* ('bouncer'), consisting of fried eggs and ham on bread.

Traditional
In the past, people needed substantial food to combat a climate that delivers lots of rain and wind. Traditional dishes include *erwtensoep* (ultra-thick pea and ham soup); *stamppot* (mashed vegetables with sausage); *hutspot* (beef stew); *boerenkool met worst* (kale with sausage); and *pannekoeken* (pancakes) with toppings that range from bacon and cheese to *stroop* (syrup) and sugar. *Patat* (french fries) are served with mayonnaise (*fritessaus*).

52

Seafood

Maatjes (raw herring) is a genuine Dutch treat, bought from street stalls, served with raw onion, and eaten whole or chopped into slices. Almost as popular is *gerookte paling* (smoked eel), traditionally from the IJsselmeer. In months with an 'r' in them, you can eat *mosselen* (mussels) and *oesters* (oysters) from the pure waters of Zeeland's Eastern Scheldt estuary. Grey North Sea prawns are popular and tasty. All kinds of other fish are available, including cod, sole, plaice, turbot, salmon and halibut, as well as Mediterranean and tropical species.

Indonesian

The Dutch East Indies were the jewel of Holland's colonial empire. In a reversal of fortunes, Indonesian cuisine has conquered the former mother country. Highlight of the menu is *rijsttafel* (rice table), a cascade of up to 20 or more dishes ranging from mild to volcanically spicy. *Rijsttafel* was invented by the colonial Dutch, and there is a tendency to look down on it as being for tourists only, yet it provides a good introduction to Indonesian cuisine. As menus often have no English translation, look for such items as *ayam* (chicken), *ikan* (fish), *telor* (egg), *rendang* (beef), *kroepoek* (shrimp crackers), *sateh* (pork kebabs in spicy peanut sauce) and *gado-gado* (vegetables in peanut sauce).

Indonesian food is popular and widely available in the city

Cheese

Round Edam and cylindrical Gouda cheeses are the best known. Try also *Leidse kaas*, flavoured with caraway seeds, and *Friese kaas*, flavoured with cloves.

Drinks

Dutch pilsener beers Heineken, Grolsch and Amstel are well known, and there are others, such as Oranjeboom, Bavaria, Brand, Gulpen, Ridder, Leeuw, Alfa and Lindeboom. For a change, try a *witbier* (white beer) such as Wiekse Witte, or a brown *bokbier*. Dutch *jenever* (gin), usually ordered as a *borreltje* (small tot), is a popular accompaniment to beer, the two forming a symbiotic relationship called a *kopstoot* ('knock on the head').

Time for a 'knock on the head' – jenever with beer

+ 40B4
✉ Between Prinsengracht,
Brouwersgracht,
Lijnbaansgracht and
Leidsegracht
🚊 1, 2, 5, 6, 7, 10, 13,
14, 17
🚢 Museum Boat stop 7

*Above: over the hump on
a bridge spanning
Keizersgracht*

+ 40B4
🍴 Bars, cafés and
restaurants (€–€€€)
🚊 1, 2, 4, 5, 6, 13, 14, 16,
17, 24, 25
🚢 Museum Boat stop 4, 7

DE JORDAAN

The Jordaan, which lies west of the centre between Prinsengracht, Brouwersgracht, Singelgracht and Leidsegracht, is a town within a town, built for Golden Age artisans and tradesmen who provided services to their 'betters' on the adjacent *grachtengordel*. Its houses are smaller and more crammed together, its waterways narrower and less grand, than those of the prestigious ring canals. The name may come from the French *jardin*, after the gardens of Protestant Huguenot refugees who lived in the area. Though infiltrated by gentrifiers, the neighbourhood retains a sense of place, and its iconoclastic working-class attitudes have been complemented by an influx of artists, designers and offbeat folks in general. With few 'sights' in the accepted sense, the Jordaan is worth visiting for its character, cafés and restaurants and individualistic shops.

KEIZERSGRACHT ✪✪✪

The Emperor's Canal is named for Emperor Maximilian of Austria, whose crown graces the Westerkerk spire (► 26), and has a wealth of gable and façade styles. Its 2.8km course takes in several sights that merit a close-up look. In its northern reaches, at Nos 40–4, are the Groenland Pakhuizen from 1641, three surviving warehouses from the original five in which the Greenland Company stored whale oil. Number 123, the Huis met de Hoofden, has six sculpted heads on the façade, representing Greek gods. Near the canal's southern end is the Museum Van Loon (► 59).

The Jordaan

Listen for the Westertoren carillon (➤ 26), a reassuring sound that has wafted over the Jordaan for centuries.

Pass the Anne Frankhuis (➤ 17) on Prinsengracht, cross the canal by the first bridge, and backtrack to Bloemgracht.

Check out three 1640s step gables at Nos 87–91, on which are carved gablestones with images of a townsman, countryman and seaman.

Take Eerste Leliedwarsstraat to Egelantiersgracht.

The hardware store at Nos 2–6 is a 1920s Amsterdam School interloper. At Nos 107–45, step through a Delft blue-tiled corridor into the 1617 Sint-Andrieshofje's courtyard garden (➤ 70), an 'oasis of peace'.

Take Eerste Egelantiersdwarsstraat to the corner of Egelantiersstraat, for the Claes Claeszoon Hofje (➤ 43). Continue on Eerste Tuindwarsstraat and Eerste Anjeliersdwarsstraat to Westerstraat.

If you are here when the Westermarkt street market is on, rummage for cheap clothes, records or household items.

Continue on Tweede Boomdwarsstraat, then turn left into Karthuizersstraat.

Numbers 11–19 are 18th-century gabled houses. The Huiszitten Weduwenhof (Nos 69–191) is a former 18th-century home for widows, with a beautiful courtyard garden. A Carthusian monastery used to stand near by.

Come out on to Lindengracht.

Visit the 1670 Suyckerhofje at Nos 149–163, and its beautifully restored courtyard garden.

Take Tweede Goudsbloemdwarsstraat, Palmdwarsstraat and Driehoekstraat to the junction of Brouwersgracht and Singelgracht.

Tranquil Egelantiersgracht – one of the Jordaan's handsome side-canals

Distance
3km

Time
1½ hours

Start point
Westermarkt
✚ 40B4
🚊 6, 13, 14, 17
⛴ Museum Boat stop 7

End point
Singelgracht
✚ 40C4
🚊 3

Lunch
De Prins (➤ 96)
Rum Runners (➤ 96)
't Smalle (➤ 114)

Westerstraat market
🕐 Mon–Sat 8–2

55

Almost an original: the wax model of Vincent van Gogh at Madame Tussaud's

40C3

✉ Dam 20

☎ 552 1010

🕐 Jul–Aug daily 9:30–8:30; Sep–Jun daily 10–6:30. Closed 30 Apr

🚋 4, 9, 14, 16, 24, 25

♿ Good

💵 Very expensive

KONINKLIJK PALEIS (► 19, TOP TEN)

LEIDSEPLEIN (► 20, TOP TEN)

MADAME TUSSAUD'S　　　　　　　　**○○**

More than a gallery of waxen Dutch stares, this waxworks uses audio-animatronics, climate-control, smell generators and other special effects to bring to life Holland from the Golden Age onwards. You will see Rembrandt, Vermeer, Jan Steen and others at work. Kings, princes, merchants and peasants put in an appearance. Walk-through scenes include an Amsterdam canalside, a brown café and ice-skating, and there are such famous Dutch characters as Erasmus, Mata Hari and Johann Cruyff, as well as international greats, including Churchill, Einstein and Gandhi.

DID YOU KNOW?

Amsterdam has an officially tabulated 1,281 bridges. You can see 15 from the bridge over Herengracht at Thorbeckeplein. Torensluis (1684), on Singel at Oude Leliestraat, is the widest. The cast-iron Blauwbrug (Blue Bridge) over the Amstel, built in 1884 and inspired by Paris's Pont Alexandre III, retains the nickname of a 16th-century wooden bridge painted 'Nassau Blue' after the 1578 religious Alteratie; having lost its blue paint in 1969, the Blauwbrug got it back in a renovation completed in 2000.

MAGERE BRUG ⭐⭐

The famous 'Skinny Bridge', a white-painted double-drawbridge, has spanned the River Amstel since 1672. The current bridge is a 1969 replacement of an 18th-century enlargement of the original, which is said to have taken its name from two wealthy sisters, called Mager, who lived on opposite banks of the Amstel and who had the bridge built to make it easier for them to visit each other. Its name more likely comes from the original bridge being so narrow that two people could barely cross at the same time. The not-so-skinny footbridge, made of African azobe wood, is the finest of the city's 60 traditional Dutch drawbridges and a big tourist draw at night, when it is lit by hundreds of lights. You might see the bicycle-borne bridge master raising it to let boats through.

41D2
Between Kerkstraat and Nieuwe Kerkstraat
4

Above: crossing the Amstel on the famous Magere Brug

MUNTTOREN ⭐⭐

The Mint Tower's base is all that remains of the 1490 Reguliers Gate in the demolished city wall. It got its present name in 1672–3, during the war with England and France, when coins were minted here. In 1620, Hendrick de Keyser, who had already topped the Montelbaanstoren, added an ornate, bell-covered spire. A tinkling carillon breaks every hour into classical, folk or pop music, and on Friday from noon until 1PM the bells play a mini-concert. The tower is closed to the public except for a ground-floor shop selling blue porcelain.

Look for a carving on the attached building, which was once a guardhouse and is now a souvenir shop, depicting Amsterdam's alternative foundation tale: the image of two men and a seasick dog in a boat (► 44).

40C3
Muntplein
4, 9, 14, 16, 24, 25

The hidden splendour of the Church of Our Lord in the Attic

Oudezijds Voorburgwal 40
624 6604
Mon–Sat 10–5, Sun and pub hols 1–5. Closed 1 Jan, 30 Apr
Centraal Station
1, 2, 4, 5, 6, 9, 13, 14, 16, 17, 24, 25
Museum Boat stop 1
None
Moderate

41D3
Jodenbreestraat 4–6
520 0400
Mon–Sat 10–5. Sun and Pub hols 1–5. Closed 1 Jan
Waterlooplein
9, 14
Museum Boat stop 3
Few
Moderate

MUSEUM AMSTELKRING

You get two museums in one here. First is the canal house, built between 1661 and 1663 by merchant Jan Hartman, who sold stockings in a ground-floor shop. Its 17th-century oak furniture, paintings and decoration give a superb idea of period life. Hartman was Catholic and, as a 1578 law prohibited Catholic services, he turned the attics of this and two adjacent houses he also owned into a *schuilkerk*, a clandestine church. Of many such churches, only this one has been completely preserved. Historians of the Amstelkring (Amstel Circle) saved it from demolition in 1888 and named it Ons' Lieve Heer op Solder (Our Lord in the Attic). You climb a narrow stairway to the third-floor church, remodelled in baroque style in 1739 and with many of its original religious objects, including Jacob de Wit's painting *The Baptism of Christ* (1736). An occasional service is still held, as are recitals.

MUSEUM HET REMBRANDTHUIS

The great Dutch artist Rembrandt van Rijn (1606–69) owned this house (built in 1606) from 1639, when his work was in constant demand, until he was forced to sell in 1658 because of bankruptcy. Restoration work, completed in 2001, has returned the house to the way it looked when Rembrandt lived and worked in it. The combined living room and bedroom, and Rembrandt's studio are highlights of the tour. His wife, Saskia van Uylenburgh, died here in 1642, aged 30, shortly after their son Titus was born in the house. You can also see paintings by his teacher, Pieter Lastman, and some of his students. Around 250 of Rembrandt's 300 surviving engravings and drawings are on display in the exhibition wing from 1998 next door, including portraits, self-portraits and landscapes.

Rembrandt's house is now a museum

MUSEUM VAN LOON ⭐⭐

Along with its neighbouring twin at No 674, this classical mansion of the fading Golden Age by architect Adriaan Dortsman was built between 1671 and 1672 for two wealthy merchant brothers. Rembrandt's student, the artist Ferdinand Bol (1616–80), lived here. The Van Loon family, whose ancestors had played a distinguished role in Holland's history, bought the house in 1884, transforming it into a museum in the 1960s. You can visit its magnificently furnished rooms, climb the marble staircase, stroll in the garden and admire a coach house in the shape of a Greek temple.

✚ 40C2
✉ Keizersgracht 672
☎ 624 5255
🕐 Sep–Jun Fri–Mon 11–5;
   Jul–Aug daily 11–5.
   Closed 1 Jan, 30 Apr, 25
   Dec
🚌 6, 24, 25
♿ None
💶 Moderate

MUSEUM WILLET-HOLTHUYSEN ⭐⭐

Another patrician canal house-turned-museum, this one was built in 1687 for a member of the city council, Jacob Hop. In 1855 Pieter Gerard Holthuysen, a glass merchant, bought it and, in due course, his daughter Sandrina and her husband, Abraham Willett, inherited the house. The couple built up a valuable collection of glass, silver, porcelain and paintings and in 1895 turned over the lot, house included, to an unenthusiastic city council for use as a museum. Following refurbishment the museum has been attracting more visitors to its 18th-century basement kitchen, Victorian bedrooms, the Blue Room, with its painted ceiling – *Dawn Chasing Away Night*, by Jacob de Wit (1744) – and dining salon with places set for a banquet.

✚ 41D2
✉ Herengracht 605
☎ 523 1822
🕐 Mon–Fri 10–5, Sat–Sun
   11–5. Closed 1 Jan, 30
   April, 25 Dec
🚌 4, 9, 14
🚢 Museum Boat stop 3
♿ None
💶 Moderate

The full-size replica of the Dutch East Indiaman Amsterdam, *moored to a wharf at the Netherlands Maritime Museum*

🚹 40C3
✉ Dam
🚌 4, 9, 14, 16, 24, 25

🚹 40A1
✉ Vondelpark 3
☎ 589 1400
🕐 Tue–Fri 10–5, Sat 11–5
🍴 Café Vertigo (€€)
🚌 1, 2, 3, 5, 6, 12
🚤 Museum Boat stop 5
♿ Good 👜 Moderate

🚹 41E3
✉ Kattenburgerplein 1
☎ 523 2222
🕐 Tue–Sun 10–5, also Mon mid-Jun–mid-Sep, School and pub hols 10–5. Closed 1 Jan, 30 Apr, 25 Dec
🍴 Café (€)
🚌 Bus 22, 32
🚤 Museum Boat stop 2
♿ Very good
👜 Expensive

NATIONAAL MONUMENT ★

The National Monument, an obelisk with symbolic sculptures, was erected in 1956 to commemorate the victims of Holland's occupation by Nazi Germany during World War II. Over the years it has become a popular meeting place.

NEDERLANDS FILMMUSEUM ★

At a 19th-century lakeside café-turned-dual-screen cinema in Vondelpark, film buffs get to see the best of historical, avant-garde and international films. Many are from the museum's own 35,000-film collection, and the movies are backed up by an extensive library and intermittent temporary exhibitions. The Café Vertigo (named after the Hitchcock movie) is a fine supporting feature, in particular for its great outdoor terrace.

NEDERLANDS SCHEEPVAARTMUSEUM ★★★

The star turn at the Netherlands Maritime Museum is the *Amsterdam* (see box), a full-size replica of a United East India Company sailing ship that ran aground and was lost off Hastings in 1749, which is tied up at the museum's wharf. From April to October its 'crew' puts on regular re-enactments of scenes from an 18th-century sailor's life. The *Amsterdam* has been joined by the *Stad Amsterdam*, a replica 19th-century iron clipper, which is moored at nearby Java Island when it's not sailing. The museum, in a 1656 Amsterdam Admiralty arsenal, is a treasure trove of this seafaring nation's long and distinguished maritime history. In addition to the two replicas you can see an ice-breaker, a lifeboat, a herring lugger, canal barges, Holland's royal barge, last used in 1962 for Queen Juliana's silver

wedding anniversary, and Greenpeace's *Rainbow Warrior*, as well as models of sailing ships, liners, warships and modern cargo vessels.

Among historical maps and charts is a bound edition of cartographer Jan Blaeu's 17th-century *World Atlas*, accompanied by marine paintings, navigational instruments, photographs, ships' equipment and other nautical bits and pieces. A particular focus is the history of the Amsterdam-based Vereenigde Oostindische Compagnie (United East India Company), founded in 1602.

The 17th-century Amsterdam Admiralty arsenal that houses the Maritime Museum

The hi-tech NEMO

DID YOU KNOW?

When the *Amsterdam* lost its rudder on a voyage to the East Indies, Captain Willem Klump beached his three-masted ship off Hastings in England. He saved his passengers and crew and recovered 28 chests of silver. Much of the cargo remains onboard: medicines, foodstuffs, wine, muskets, cannon and munitions. With its upper decks washed away and its hull visible at very low tide, the *Amsterdam* lies embedded in sand.

NEMO ✪✪

Technology and science are the related themes at this interactive museum housed in a spectacular, modern building from 1997 by Italian architect Renzo Piano in Amsterdam harbour. NEMO brings you face to face with the latest developments through such hands-on virtual activities as steering a supertanker, trading shares, generating power and performing surgery. You can conduct scientific experiments in a laboratory, do basic research on natural phenomena, play computer games, watch tech-oriented demonstrations, movies and theatre performances, listen to debates, surf the web and tour temporary exhibitions. The rooftop terrace has become a popular spot for soaking up sun and watching the sunset.

➕ 41E4
✉ Oosterdok 2
☎ 0900 919 1100
🕐 Jul–Aug daily 10–5; Sep–Jun Tue–Sun 10–5. Closed 1 Jan, 30 Apr, 25 Dec
🍽 Café with waterside terrace (€); cafeteria with rooftop terrace (€–€€)
🚌 Bus 22, 32
🚢 Museum Boat stop 2
♿ Very good
💶 Very expensive

Refurbished and revived, Nieuwmarkt is awash with restaurants and cafés

<table>
<tr><td>✚</td><td>40C4</td></tr>
<tr><td>✉</td><td>Dam</td></tr>
<tr><td>☎</td><td>638 6909</td></tr>
<tr><td>🕐</td><td>Daily 10–6 (Thu until 10 during exhibitions)</td></tr>
<tr><td>🍴</td><td>Nieuwe Café (€€)</td></tr>
<tr><td>🚌</td><td>1, 2, 4, 5, 6, 9, 13, 14, 16, 17, 24, 25</td></tr>
<tr><td>♿</td><td>Very good</td></tr>
<tr><td>🎫</td><td>Free (special exhibitions range from moderate to very expensive)</td></tr>
</table>

NIEUWE KERK ✪✪

The New Church has been Holland's coronation church since 1815, but is now mostly used for art exhibitions and cultural events. It dates from 1408, though an original Gothic structure was destroyed by fire in 1521. Calvinists stripped out the Catholic ornamentation after their 1578 take-over. Where the high altar once stood is an elaborate marble memorial to Admiral Michiel de Ruyter (1607–76), who in 1667 singed the King of England's beard by sailing up the Medway and destroying an English fleet. Sculpted by Rombout Verhulst, it depicts the hero lying on a cannon, surrounded by sea creatures. Poets Pieter Cornelisz Hooft (1581–1647) and Joost van den Vondel (1587–1679) are buried in the church in unmarked graves.

<table>
<tr><td>✚</td><td>41D3</td></tr>
<tr><td>🍴</td><td>Many cafés (€) and restaurants (€–€€)</td></tr>
<tr><td>Ⓜ</td><td>Nieuwmarkt</td></tr>
</table>

NIEUWMARKT ✪✪

A seedy area well into the 1980s, where heroin addicts and ne'er-do-wells hung out, the market square's character was appropriate, as this was once the site of public executions, and bits and pieces of dismembered criminals were hung up on De Waag (➤ 73) as a warning to others. Having been cleaned up, more or less, it is becoming a popular, alternative nightlife zone. At the heart of the city's Chinatown, it has many authentic, inexpensive Chinese eateries, as well as good traditional Dutch cafés with pavement terraces. Just off the square, on Zeedijk, is the new Buddist Fo Guang Shan He Hua Temple, a remarkable sight on this bustling street.

NOORDERKERK ✪

The austere North Church, renovated between 1997 and 1998, is a rarity in this nominally Calvinist city: a Calvinist church with a substantial congregation. It was built in the shape of a Greek cross by Hendrick de Keyser, and completed in 1623 by Hendrick Staets after De Keyser's death in 1621. Staets tucked four little triangular houses into the angles of the cross. Surrounding Noordermarkt hosts a bird market and organic food market on Saturday with stalls selling fruit and vegetables, herbs and cheeses, and a flea market on Monday.

🕂 40B4
✉ Noordermarkt 44–8
☎ 626 6436
🕓 Sat 11–1 (followed by chamber music concert 1–2), Sun services 10AM and 7PM, Mon 10:30–12:30. Closed Tue–Fri
🚌 Bus 18, 22
♿ Few
💷 Free

OOSTINDISCH HUIS ✪

This is the former headquarters of the once-powerful Veerenigde Oostindische Compagnie (United East India Company), which was founded in 1602. Its occupants once sent expeditions to the Orient to bring back silks, spices and other riches that fuelled Amsterdam's Golden Age. They controlled their own army and had authority to declare war and make treaties. Hendrick de Keyser's red brick and yellow sandstone building, dating from 1605–6, now belongs to Amsterdam University; you can stroll into its courtyard, and by pretending to be a student can peruse the interior.

🕂 41D3
✉ Oude Hoogstraat 24
🚋 4, 9, 14, 16, 24, 25

Oude Kerk is an island of piety in the Red Light District

OUDE KERK ✪✪

The Gothic Old Church, begun in 1334, stands in the heart of the Red Light District, surrounded by former almshouses. In summer you can climb the spire, built by Joost Bilhamer in 1555, and on Saturday between 4 and 5PM the carillon bursts into tune. Not much Catholic ornamentation survived the Calvinist takeover, but in the Mariakapel you can see three superb stained-glass windows. Composer Jan Sweelinck (1562–1621) is buried in the church where he was organist for 45 years, as are Rembrandt's wife Saskia, a squadron of 17th-century admirals and poet Maria Tesselschade, who died in 1649.

🕂 41D4
✉ Oudekerksplein 23
☎ 625 8284
🕓 Church: Mon–Sat 11–5, Sun 1–5. Tower: Jun–Sep Wed–Sun 2–4; Sep–Apr Sun–Fri 1–5, Sat 11–5. Closed 1 Jan, 30 Apr
🚇 Nieuwmarkt
🚋 4, 9, 14, 16, 24, 25
♿ Good
💷 Moderate

Old Centre

Distance
3km

Time
2 hours

Start point
Rokin, at Spui
🚇 40C3
🚌 4, 9, 14, 16, 24, 25

End point
Dam
🚇 40C3
🚌 4, 9, 14, 16, 24, 25

Lunch
Café Roux (► 93)
La Ruche (► 96)

Flirt with the salacious on a stroll through De Wallen, and find there is more to the oldest part of town than sleaze.

Walk past a canal boat dock and a statue of Queen Wilhelmina, into Lange Brugsteeg and Grimburgwal, to Oudezijds Voorburgwal.

You're on Amsterdam University's downtown campus. On the corner in front of you is a 16th-century red-brick, step-gabled house with a view of three canals. To your left, on Oudezijds Voorburgwal, is the Athenaeum Illustre (► 38).

Cross over the canal to Oudezijds Achterburg-wal. Directly ahead is Oudemanhuispoort, a covered passage lined with second-hand book stalls (► 65). Go through and turn left on Kloveniersburgwal.

Across the water, at No 95, you see the neo-classical Poppenhuis, built in the 1640s for merchant Joan Poppen.

Continue to Oude Hoogstraat and turn left to visit the courtyard of Oostindisch Huis (► 63). Return to Kloveniersburgwal and turn left.

The Oude Kerk organ, once played by composer Jan Sweelinck

Across the water, at No 29, is the neo-classical Trippen-huis, built between 1660 and 1664 by Justus Vingboons for the arms merchant Trip brothers – with chimneys shaped like cannon barrels. It is actually two houses, one for each of the brothers, disguised by false middle windows to maintain its symmetry. The building is now home to the Netherlands Academy. You pass tiny Klein-Trippenhuis, built for their coachman, at No 26 (► 71).

Keep going to Nieuwmarkt and De Waag (► 73). Take Zeedijk, then turn left on Molensteeg into the heart of the Red Light District (► 21). Keep going across the two canals until you come to the Oude Kerk (► 63).

Prostitutes' red-lit windows surround the church.

Take Wijde Kerksteeg, then turn left on Warmoesstraat, to the Dam.

OUDEMANHUISPOORT

Once the entrance to a hospice for elderly men, this long covered passage dating from 1601 beside Amsterdam University now houses antiquarian and second-hand book stalls that spread their wares on tables lining the arcade. Midway along, on either side, are doors that open onto Amsterdam University's law department buildings; the doors on the left lead first to a courtyard garden with a sculpted head of Minerva in the middle.

40C3
Mon–Sat 10–5/6
4, 9, 14, 16, 24, 25

PORTUGEES-ISRAËLIETISCHE SYNAGOGE ⊗

Sephardic Jews fleeing persecution in Spain and Portugal began to settle in Amsterdam during the 1580s, bringing a touch of colour to the sober, Calvinist city. As a sign of their prosperity in a relatively tolerant environment, they pooled their wealth to build the lavish Portuguese-Israelite Synagogue (1671–5), designed by Elias Bouman. Wooden barrel vaults supported on Ionic columns form the interior, which is decorated with low-hanging brass chandeliers.

41D3
Mr Visserplein 1
624 5351
Apr–Oct Sun–Fri 10–6;
Nov–Mar Sun–Thu 10–6,
Fri 10–3. Closed Sat &
Jewish hols (except for
services)
Waterlooplein
9, 14
Museum Boat stop 5
Good
Moderate

Knick-knacks and souvenir shops on Prinsengracht

PRINSENGRACHT ⊗⊗⊗

Prinsengracht, the outermost of the three concentric ring canals, was named after Prince William of Orange. It was dug in the 17th century to house shopkeepers and craftsmen. With the stiffly formal patricians' and merchants' houses reserved for Herengracht (➤ 47) and Keizersgracht (➤ 54), Prinsengracht's down-to-earth style has survived the centuries. A stroll along its houseboat-lined, 3.5km length and into adjacent side-streets, particularly in the northern section bordering the Jordaan (➤ 54), takes you past cosy brown cafés, notable restaurants and offbeat shops and boutiques. Highlights of its course through the city are the Anne Frankhuis (➤ 17) and Westerkerk (➤ 26); also visit the Noorderkerk (➤ 63) and the canal's junction with Brouwersgracht (➤ 42).

40B4
Many cafés and restaurants (€–€€€)
1, 2, 4, 5, 6, 7, 10, 13, 14, 16, 17, 24, 25
Museum Boat stop 2

PRINSENHOF

The Prince's House was the St Cecilia Convent until the 1578 Protestant *Alteratie*, when the city commandeered it as a lodging house. In 1647, the Admiralty moved in, and when, in 1808, Louis Napoleon turfed the city councillors out of their town hall on the Dam, they moved here. Since the council left in 1986, the Prinsenhof has become the Grand Hotel, a predominantly 1920s Amsterdam School structure. In its Café Roux (➤ 93), you can see a 1949 mural, *Inquisitive Children*, by Cobra artist Karel Appel.

RED LIGHT DISTRICT (➤ 21, TOP TEN)

REMBRANDTPLEIN

Brash and bustling Rembrandtplein jumps at night with music from the mostly unmemorable cafés that surround it (see side panel for three exceptions). A bronze statue of Rembrandt (1852) by Louis Royer, in the middle of the square, doesn't look much like the down-at-heel self-portraits the artist typically painted. While you're here, visit the magnificent, art deco Tuschinski Cinema (1921) at adjacent Reguliersbreestraat 26 – you can wander around the lobby, and in July and August join guided tours.

Rembrandt occupies pride of place in the square that bears his name

---

Side panel (Prinsenhof):

✚ 40C3
✉ Oudezijds Voorburgwal 197
☎ 555 3111
🍴 Café Roux (€€)
🚌 4, 9, 14, 16, 24, 25

Side panel (Rembrandtplein):

✚ 40C2
🍴 Café Schiller (€–€€); Grand Café l'Opera (€–€€); Royal Café de Kroon (€–€€)
🚌 4, 9, 14, 16, 24, 25
❓ Guided tours Sun and Mon at 10:30

DE RIEKER ✪

Amsterdam's finest windmill stands amid idyllic surroundings beside the River Amstel and Amstelpark (► 33) in the city's leafy southern outskirts. Built in 1636 to drain the Rieker polder (low-lying reclaimed land), the windmill was moved here in the 1970s. It has been beautifully preserved and is now a private home. Rembrandt walked in this tranquil area after his wife's death, sketching and painting riverside scenes, and a statue of the artist at work stands beside the windmill.

RIJKSMUSEUM (► 22–3, TOP TEN)

RONDVAARTBOTEN ✪✪✪

Many visitors prefer not to board a canal boat. Don't be one of them. True, there's a lot of tourist hokum associated with these glass-topped cruisers but you can ignore that, more or less, and focus on the unmatched view you get of this canal-threaded city from the water, gliding past a parade of Golden Age gables enlivened by contemporary bustle and colour.

Nine tour-boat companies (► side panel) sail from jetties around the city centre – at Centraal Station, along Damrak and Rokin, at Leidseplein and on Singelgracht at Weteringplantsoen.

Most cruises last about an hour and follow a similar pattern: through the ring canals and the old city, around the Red Light District, taking in the River Amstel and a circuit of Centraal Station along the way. There are longer cruises on the river and through the old harbour, as well as dinner- and cheese-and-wine-cruises.

Variations on the tour boat theme are the Canal Bus, Museum Boat and water-taxis, as well as 'saloon boat' tours on refurbished motor launches dating from the 1890s to the 1920s. And although it's not quite the same thing, you can be captain of your own 'ship' and tour the waterways by water bike (► 42). Remember that boat traffic keeps to the right-hand side of the canal.

✚ 29D1
⊠ Corner of Amsteldijk and De Borcht
🍴 't Klein Kalfje (► 94)
🚌 Bus 148

❓ Canal boat tours are operated by:
Amsterdam Canal Cruises ☎ 626 5636
Holland International ☎ 622 7788
Meijers Rondvaarten ☎ 623 4208
Rederij Boekel ☎ 612 9905
Rederij Hof van Holland ☎ 623 7122
Rederij Lovers ☎ 530 1090
Rederij Noord-Zuid ☎ 679 1370
Rederij P Kooij ☎ 623 3810
Rederij Plas ☎ 624 5406

Cruiseboat is the best way to travel

From shipping company headquarters to city transport offices – Scheepvaarthuis

---

➕ 41D4
✉ Prins Hendrikkade 108–114
🕐 Mon–Fri 9–4:30
🚇 Centraal Station
🚌 Bus 22, 32, 33, 34, 35, 39

➕ 41D4
✉ Prins Hendrikkade 94–5
🍴 VOC Café (€)
🚇 Centraal Station
🚊 Tram 1, 2, 4, 5, 9, 13, 16, 17, 24, 25; bus 22, 32
🚢 Museum Boat stop 1

➕ 40C3
✉ Kalverstraat 92, Nieuwezijds Voorburgwal 359, Sint-Luciënsteeg 27
☎ 523 1822
🕐 Mon–Fri 10–5, Sat–Sun and pub hols 11–5
🚊 1, 2, 4, 5, 9, 14, 16, 24, 25
🚢 Museum Boat stop 4
♿ Very good 👋 Free

SCHEEPVAARTHUIS ⭐

Maritime House, noted for its curving lines and marine motifs, is a work of the Amsterdam School, which flowered briefly early this century. Designed by Michel de Klerk, Pieter Kramer and Johan van der May between 1912 and 1913 for a consortium of local shipping companies, it now houses the city's municipal transport authority, the GVB. It is ornamented with portrait busts of famous captains, navigators and cartographers. Near by, at Prins Hendrikkade 131, is a house that once belonged to the 17th-century admiral, Michiel de Ruyter.

SCHREIERSTOREN ⭐⭐

The Weeping Tower began life around 1480 as a heavily fortified strong point in the city wall overlooking the harbour. Its somewhat fanciful name comes from the tears sailors' wives and sweethearts ostensibly shed from its ramparts as ships sailed away on long and often fatal voyages to the East and West Indies. A plaque on the wall shows such an apparently distraught woman watching a ship depart. Other plaques on the tower record Henry Hudson's 1609 voyage to what was to be known as New York and the Hudson River, and Cornelis Houtman's 1595 voyage to Indonesia; both expeditions left from the harbour here.

SCHUTTERSGALERIJ ⭐⭐

The Civic Guards Gallery, belonging to the Amsterdams Historisch Museum (► 16), displays 15 vast 16th- and 17th-century group portraits of the city's Civic Guards, local militia companies. They are hung in a covered passageway that was once a narrow canal separating the boys' and girls' courtyards of the former orphanage (now housing the Historical Museum). One of the canvases on display is *Joan Huydecoper's Militia Celebrating the Peace of Münster* (1648), which was painted by Rembrandt's student Govert Flinck.

SEXMUSEUM AMSTERDAM VENUSTEMPEL ✪

Once you get past the 'cultural' stuff, a false marble entrance in the shape of a classical pediment, you're into the Sex Museum's serious business, which ranges from naughty to downright dirty. Erotic photographs and videos show practitioners at work on diverse forms of interpersonal relationships. Mannequins are used to bring you close to the 'action'. Other exhibits include toys, trinkets, specialised clothing and appliances.

SINGEL ✪✪✪

Before the city embarked on its Golden Age expansion, this canal formed a moat outside the walls. By the early 17th century it was a residential zone and the earliest ring canal. There are few major monuments on its 1.7km course through the city between Prins Hendrikkade, near Centraal Station, and the Munttoren (➤ 57), beside the Flower Market (➤ 39), yet a stroll along its length is full of minor interest. The Nieuwe Haarlemmersluis beside Brouwersgracht, an outlet from the canals, plays an important part in the 1½-hour 'enema' the system gets every night, when fresh water is pumped through to flush the canals out. Near here, moored beside Singel 40, is the *Poezenboot*, a refuge for dozens of stray cats. The Torensluis at Oude Leliestraat is the city's widest bridge.

Among Singel's most interesting churches is the Ronde Lutherse Koepelkerk (Round Domed Lutheran Church), built between 1668 and 1671 by Adriaen Dortsman for the city's Lutheran community and now used by the Renaissance Amsterdam Hotel as a conference centre.

✚	41D4
✉	Damrak 18
☎	622 8376
🕐	Daily 10AM–11:30PM
Ⓜ	Centraal Station
🚌	1, 2, 4, 5, 6, 9, 13, 16, 17, 24, 25
🚢	Museum Boat stop 1
♿	Few Inexpensive
❓	No admission to under-16s

✚	40C4
🍴	Cafés and restaurants (€–€€€)
🚌	1, 2, 4, 5, 6, 9, 13, 14, 16, 17, 24, 25
🚢	Museum Boat stop 1, 4

Nieuwe Haarlemmersluis gives access to and from the Singel

🎫 40C4
🚌 1, 2, 5, 6, 13, 17

SINGEL 7 ✪

Canal boat tour guides point out the façade of this 16th-century house as the city's narrowest, at 1m wide – an important consideration in times past, as the wider the canal frontage, the more a building cost. Singel 7 cleverly uses a narrow frontage then widens to a more usual size behind the façade.

🎫 40B4
✉ Egelantiersgracht 107–45
🚌 7, 10, 17

SINT-ANDRIESHOFJE ✪

Bequeathed in 1615–17 by cattle farmer Ivo Gerrittszoon, this restored almshouse still forms a social housing unit. A corridor lined with Delft blue tiles leads to a courtyard garden, filled with flowers and containing a water pump and a dedication stone with the legend *Vrede Sy Met U* (Peace Be With You).

🎫 41D4
✉ Prins Hendrikkade 73
☎ 624 8749
🕐 Mon–Sat 11–4; Sun services
Ⓒ Centraal Station
🚌 1, 2, 4, 5, 6, 9, 13, 16, 17, 24, 25
🚢 Museum Boat stop 1
♿ Good
✋ Free

SINT-NICOLAASKERK ✪

With its twin towers and tall, domed cupola, the city's main Catholic church (1888), dedicated to St Nicholas, is a highly visible landmark facing Centraal Station. Recently restored, the church's richly decorated interior is almost neo-baroque, its square pillars topped with Corinthian capitals. The marble high altar is flanked by bronze reliefs recalling the 1345 Miracle of Amsterdam: on the right Emperor Maximilian gives Amsterdam the imperial crown after being cured of illness following a visit to the Sacrament Chapel; on the left is a depiction of the Miracle Procession. In addition to being the patron saint of Amsterdam and sailors, St Nicholas is Sinterklaas, Holland's traditional version of Santa Claus, who on the night of 5 December – *Sinterklaasavond*, or *Pakjesavond* – delivers presents to sleeping children.

Puzzling over the meanings at the modern art Stedelijk Museum

STEDELIJK MUSEUM CS   ✪✪✪

The modern art Municipal Museum's building at Museumplein, which opened in 1895, and its new wing from 1954 are both closed until some time in 2006 for major refurbishment. In the meantime, the museum has taken up temporary quarters in the TPG Gebouw Building close to Centraal Station.

Things change fast at the Stedelijk and you never know what will be on view. The permanent collection includes De Stijl works by Piet Mondrian, Cobra by Karel Appel and abstract expressionism by Willem de Kooning. Among many other artists represented are Calder, Cézanne, Chagall, Manet, Monet, Oldenburg, Picasso, Renoir, Rosenquist, Van Gogh and Warhol, and there's also a large collection of abstract paintings by Russian artist Kasimir Malevich. There is strong public demand to view the Stedelijk's works from around 1900 until the 1970s, while the healthy private galleries scene in the city allows the very latest art to be viewed elsewhere.

✚	40D4
✉	TPG Gebouw (Building), Oosterdokskade 3–5
☎	573 2911
⏱	Daily 11–5. Closed 1 Jan, 30 Apr, 25 Dec
🚉	Centraal Station
🚌	1, 2, 4, 5, 6, 13, 16, 17,24
⛴	Museum Boat stop 1
♿	Moderate
✋	Moderate

STEDELIJK MUSEUM BUREAU AMSTERDAM   ✪

The decision by the Stedelijk Museum to focus on displaying modern art up to about the 1970s has left space in its coverage – or a window of opportunity – between that decade and the present which this 'offspring' gallery is designed to fill. It does so by focusing on contemporary painting, sculpture, video works, installations and performance art, mainly by young Dutch artists.

✚	B4
✉	Rozenstraat 59
☎	422 0471
⏱	Tue–Sun, pub hols 11–5. Closed 1 Jan, 30 Apr, 25 Dec
🚌	6, 13, 14, 17
♿	Moderate
✋	Free

> ### DID YOU KNOW?
>
> The Klein Trippenhuis at Kloveniersburgwal 26, which has a façade 2.44m wide, was built in 1696 for the coachman of the merchant Trip brothers (▶ 64), whose own house, at Kloveniersburgwal 29, is 22m wide. One of the brothers apparently overheard the coachman saying how he wished he had a house as wide as his masters' door, and the lucky servant had his wish fulfilled. Nowadays it's a trendy fashion boutique.

Above: *modern sculpture outside the Stedelijk Museum's temporarily closed home base*

Costume pieces take centre stage at the Theatermuseum

THEATERMUSEUM ⭐⭐

Housed in a 1638 canalside mansion designed by Philips Vingboons, with 18th-century painted ceilings by Jacob de Wit and other artists, the museum is a storehouse of Dutch and international theatre, as well as a fine example of a patrician canal house. You can see a miniature stage, costumes, models, masks, puppets, photographs, paintings and theatrical backdrops. The Netherlands Theatre Institute occupies offices in the adjacent four canal houses, including the Bartolotti House at No 170–2, built in 1618 by Hendrick de Keyser, which also has ceilings by De Wit, and others.

TORENSLUIS ⭐

The widest bridge in the old town stands on the site of a 17th-century sluice gate flanked by twin towers that were demolished in 1829. Its foundations were used for what must have been a particularly damp and gloomy prison. Today, outdoor terraces encroach onto the bridge from nearby cafés. The bronze statue is of Multatuli (Eduard Douwes Dekker), a 19th-century author.

TRAMMUSEUM AMSTERDAM ⭐

Not only has this museum, housed in the old Haarlemmermeerstation, preserved some of Amsterdam's antique trams, it has also gathered up venerable trams from other European cities. On Sundays in summer, one of these old bone-shakers sees action on the Museum Tramlijn, a 6km line that runs from the station southwards through the Amsterdamse Bos (➤ 33) to Bovenkerk.

✚ 40C4
✉ Herengracht 168
☎ 551 3300
◷ Tue–Fri 11–5, Sat–Sun & pub hols 1–5. Closed 1 Jan, 30 Apr, 25 Dec
🍴 Café (€)
🚌 6, 13, 14, 17
🚤 Museum Boat stop 7
♿ Few
 Moderate

✚ C4
✉ Singel (at Oude Leliestraat)
🚌 1, 2, 5, 6, 13, 17

✚ 28C2
✉ Amstelveenseweg 264
☎ 673 7538
◷ Easter–Aug Sun and pub hols 10:30–5:20; Jun–Jul also Sat 8–10PM
🚌 16, 24 ♿ None
 Moderate

72

TROPENMUSEUM   ✪✪✪

You might not be surprised to hear an Indonesian gamelan orchestra in Amsterdam – Indonesia was a Dutch colony, after all – but how about visiting an Arab bazaar, a Bombay slum or a Bangladeshi village? You will find them all, and more, at the outstanding Tropical Museum. Though built between 1916 and 1926 as a paean of praise to Holland's empire in the East and West Indies, in the 1970s it refocused on culture, crafts and environment in the developing world. A hands-on, walk-through, realistic style makes for a fun-filled and educational visit. Imaginative temporary exhibitions and performances of non-Western music are held in the lofty, galleried main hall. Visiting the Kindermuseum TM Junior gives six- to 12-year-olds an insight into how people from other cultures live.

VAN GOGH MUSEUM (► 24, TOP TEN)

VONDELPARK (► 25, TOP TEN)

WAAG   ✪

Built in 1488, the moated and fortified Sint-Antoniespoort gateway in the city walls was converted into a weigh-house and guild headquarters in 1617. Rembrandt's *The Anatomy Lesson of Dr Tulp* (1632), depicting a dissection by Surgeon's Guild members, was painted here in the preserved upper floor Theatrum Anatomicum. With the city walls long vanished and the moat filled in to form Nieuwmarkt, the Waag now houses a multimedia foundation, and has a fine café-restaurant, In de Waag, on the ground floor.

✚ 41F2
✉ Linnaeusstraat 2
☎ 568 8200; Kindermuseum (reservations recommended) 568 8233
🕐 Daily 10–5 (until 3pm 5, 24, 31 Dec). Closed 1 Jan, 30 Apr, 5 May, 25 Dec.
🍴 Café-restaurant Ekeko (€–€€)
🚌 7, 9, 10, 14
♿ Very good
🖐 Expensive

Above: *exhibits from far-flung places at the Tropenmuseum*

✚ 41D3
✉ Nieuwmarkt
☎ 557 9898
🕐 Rarely open to the public (except café-restaurant)
🍴 Café-restaurant (► 97)
Ⓜ Nieuwmarkt
🚌 4, 9, 14, 16, 24, 25
♿ Few
🖐 Free (charge for some exhibitions)

WATERLOOPLEIN ⭐⭐

Once the heart of Amsterdam's Jewish Quarter, the square and its surroundings have been brutalized by successive 'development' projects since the end of the war, when it lay in ruins. A spark of the old life survives in the Waterlooplein Vlooienmarkt (flea market), which may have lost the legendary colour of its Jewish heyday, but retains the charm intrinsic to a market that retails everything from valuable antiques to worthless trash (▶ 106). The umbilically joined 1980s, postmodern Stadhuis (Town Hall) and Muziektheater (Opera), occupy the centre of the square. Between the two is the Normaal Amsterdams Peil (Amsterdam Ordnance Datum), a bronze plaque that sets Europe's altitude standard; one of the three water-filled glass columns beside it shows the high-water mark of the 1953 Zeeland floods.

WERF 'T KROMHOUT ⭐

The 18th-century Kromhout Wharf, one of the city's oldest dockyards, and among few still in business, runs a museum alongside its day-to-day operations. The shipyard was founded in the 18th century by Diede Jansen Kromhout. You can watch old canal boats being repaired and see a collection of ship's engines.

WESTERKERK (▶ 26, TOP TEN)

WESTINDISCH HUIS ⭐

Opened in 1615 as a meat market, in 1623 this became headquarters of the Dutch West India Company, which controlled Holland's trade with the Americas. In the same year the company built a settlement on Manhattan Island and in 1626 founded Nieuw Amsterdam (New York),

---

✚ 41D3
✉ Waterlooplein
🕐 Mon–Fri 9–5, Sat 8:30–5:30
🍴 Grand Café Dantzig (€€)
Ⓦ Waterlooplein
🚊 9, 14
🚌 Museum Boat stop 3
❓ Waterlooplein flea market Mon–Sat 9–5

Above: Waterlooplein flea market has all the knick-knacks you need

✚ 41F3
✉ Hoogte Kadijk 147
☎ 627 6777
🕐 Tue 10–3
🚌 Bus 22, 28
💷 Inexpensive

✚ 40C5
✉ Herenmarkt (entrance at Haarlemmerstraat 75)
🚊 Tram 1, 2, 5, 6, 13, 17; bus 18, 22

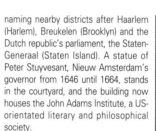

naming nearby districts after Haarlem (Harlem), Breukelen (Brooklyn) and the Dutch republic's parliament, the Staten-Generaal (Staten Island). A statue of Peter Stuyvesant, Nieuw Amsterdam's governor from 1646 until 1664, stands in the courtyard, and the building now houses the John Adams Institute, a US-orientated literary and philosophical society.

WOONBOOTMUSEUM ✪✪

If you've ever wondered what life is like aboard the city's 2,500 houseboats moored on the canals, the River Amstel and in the harbour, the Houseboat Museum is your chance to find out – though as houseboats are as individual as the people who live on them, it can only be an example rather than typical.

The 23m *Hendrika Maria*, built in 1914, was a working canal barge before being converted to a houseboat. Its hold is now living space, together with the deckhouse where the skipper and his family lived. You can tour these quarters, which have ship models and photographs on view. As with most houseboats, there is no shortage of living space but it's hard to stand up straight.

✚	40B3
✉	Beside Prinsengracht 296
☎	427 0750
🕐	Mar–Oct Wed–Sun 11–5; Nov–Dec, Feb Fri–Sun 11–5. Closed Jan, 30 Apr, 25–27 Dec
🚃	6, 13, 14, 17
🚤	Museum Boat stop 7
♿	None
💷	Inexpensive

ZUIDERKERK ✪✪

Built by Hendrick de Keyser between 1603 and 1614, the city's first, new, post-Reformation Protestant church has not been used for religious purposes since 1929. It now houses the municipal town planning information centre and an exhibition on recent and proposed urban development. At certain times you can climb the Italianate church's ornate bell tower, the Zuidertoren, for a magnificent view over the Nieuwmarkt and Waterloo-plein districts. The church-yard, where Rembrandt's first three children were buried, has been paved over and surrounded by modern apartments, but De Keyser's Renaissance gateway, 'decorated' with carved skulls, still stands beside Sint-Antoniesbreestraat.

✚	41D3
✉	Zuiderkerkhof
☎	552 7977
🕐	Mon–Fri 9–4, Sat 12–4. Church tower guided tour: Jun–Sep Wed–Sat 2, 3 & 4PM
🚇	Nieuwmarkt, Waterlooplein
🚃	9, 14
🚤	Museum Boat stop 3
♿	Good
💷	Free (church tower inexpensive)

Time has run out on Zuiderkerk's religious calling

Excursions from the City

The Netherlands is a small country. From Amsterdam you can reach its furthest mainland extremities in about three hours by way of vigorous driving or an intercity train. Within easy reach of the capital, a variety of excellent excursion options awaits you. A mere 15 minutes by train from Centraal Station is Haarlem, a memorable city in its own right, and it would be hard to imagine urban experiences more varied than those offered by The Hague, Rotterdam and Utrecht. If you need to be beside water you can choose from a string of North Sea beach resorts, such as nearby Zandvoort, or the constellation of historic towns and villages encircling the IJsselmeer lake, the former Zuiderzee. You can tour around by bicycle within a fair radius of the city, or cycle to your chosen place of escape and return by train.

'…the Dutch landscape has all the qualities that make geometry so delightful. A tour in Holland is a tour through the first book of Euclid. Over a country that is the ideal plane surface of the geometry books, the roads and the canals trace out the shortest distances between point and point.'

ALDOUS HUXLEY
Along the Road (1925)

———————————•———————————

The picturesque Kinderdijk windmills near Rotterdam

Legmeerdijk 313, Aalsmeer

0297/392 185

Mon–Fri 7:30–11. Closed 1 Jan, 31 Dec (and variably on other public holidays)

Moderate

Get there early to see the best of the auction

Below: *cheese carriers at Alkmaar cheese market*

Waagplein

Mid-Apr to mid-Sep Fri 10–12

Hollands Kaasmuseum

De Waag, Waagplein 2

072/511 4284

Apr–Oct Mon–Thu & Sat 10–4, Fri 9–4

Inexpensive

AALSMEER BLOEMENVEILING ✪✪

Flowers are big business at Aalsmeer's Flower Auction, 12km southwest of Amsterdam, where 19 million cut flowers and 2 million potted plants from 8,000 nurseries, change hands every day, representing an anuual turnover of €1.5 billion. The bidding process is highly automated and lightning fast. Dealers sit at consoles in four auditoriums, in front of big clocks with numbers from 100 to 1 on their dials. As flower and plant lots move past, the clock hand counts downwards. The first dealer to press his console button makes the highest bid, stopping the clock and securing the lot.

ALKMAAR KAASMARKT ✪✪

The Cheese Market at Alkmaar, 37km northwest of Amsterdam, is a slice of Dutch kitsch, but no less endearing for that. Every Friday morning in summer, cobblestoned Waagplein is littered with heaps of round Edam and cylindrical Gouda cheeses ready for auction. Buyers and sellers taste and haggle, sealing agreements with a clap of their hands. White-clad *kaasdragers* (cheese-porters), whose four different guild companies are identified by red, blue, yellow and green straw-hats, put the sold cheese lots on shoulder-slung wooden barrows and run with them to the Waag (Weigh House), a 14th-century church converted in 1582. You can visit the **Hollands Kaasmuseum** (Dutch Cheese Museum) in the Waag.

Keukenhof Garden

Stationsweg 166A, Lisse

0252/465 555

Late Mar–late May daily 8–6 (visitors in by 6 can stay until 7:30)

Very good

Very expensive

BOLLENSTREEK AND KEUKENHOF ✪✪✪

Tulip mania strikes the Bulb District between Haarlem and Leiden every spring. Field upon field of tulips stretches to the wide Dutch horizon. Polders (reclaimed land) become parade-grounds for a vast army of flowers, lined up in orderly regiments, each variety identified by its distinctive colour and shape – with an occasional lost recruit, a speck of red in a sea of yellow maybe, marooned in the wrong bunch. You can tiptoe through the tulips on bus tours, boat tours, taxi tours, train tours, bicycle tours, walking tours and aerial tours.

The world-famous **Keukenhof Garden**, near Lisse,

35km southwest of Amsterdam, in the heart of the bulb district, is overrun by 700,000 visitors in a two-month period in spring. These are vastly outnumbered by 7million flowers, mostly tulips, daffodils and hyacinths, but including other species, planted by Dutch flower growers in a different layout each year to showcase their products and skills.

DELFT ⭐⭐⭐

Home of the painter Jan Vermeer (1632–75) and burial place of Dutch royalty, Delft, 56km southwest of Amsterdam, is a handsome, canal-lined town. Few of its medieval buildings survived a fire in 1536 and a massive explosion at a powder magazine in 1654. Prince William the Silent, who led Holland's revolt against Spain and was assassinated in 1584 at the **Prinsenhof** – now a museum where you can still see bullet holes from the fusillade that killed him – is among members of the House of Oranje-Nassau buried in the 14th-century Nieuwe Kerk. Vermeer is buried in the 13th-century Oude Kerk. You can visit the workshop of **De Koninklijke Porcelyne Fles**, renowned makers of traditional, hand-painted Delft blue porcelain.

> ### DID YOU KNOW?
>
> German singer-songwriter Klaus-Günter Neumann wrote that quintessentially 'Dutch' song *Tulips from Amsterdam* in 1956. Postcards now take the cliché a step further, by showing a pair of sticky red lips and the slogan 'Two Lips From Amsterdam'.

🛈 Hippolytusbuurt 4
☎ 015/215 4051
🕐 Apr–Oct Mon–Sat
9–5:30, Sun 11–3;
Nov–Mar Mon–Fri
9–5:30, Sat 9–5

Prinsenhof Museum
✉ Sint-Agathaplein 1
☎ 015/260 2358
🕐 Tue–Sat 10–5, Sun & pub
hols 1–5. Closed 1 Jan,
25 Dec
👆 Inexpensive

**De Koninklijke
Porcelyne Fles**
✉ Rotterdamseweg 196
☎ 015/251 2030
🕐 Guided tours Mon–Sat
9–5; also Sun (Apr–late
Oct) 9:30–5. Closed 25
Dec–1 Jan
👆 Inexpensive

There's more to Edam than cheese – enjoy a stroll along the elegant canal banks

ℹ Stadhuis, Damplein 1
☎ 0299/315 125
◷ May–Oct Mon–Sat 10–5; Nov–Apr Mon–Sat 10–3

Edams Museum
✉ Damplein 8
☎ 0299/372 644
◷ Apr–Oct Tue–Sat 10–4:30, Sun 1–4:30
✦ Inexpensive

ℹ Markt 27 **☎** 0900/468 3288 **◷** Mon–Sat 9–5 (Nov–Mar Sat 10–4; also Jun–Aug Sun 12–5)

Stadhuis
✉ Markt
☎ 0182/588 758
◷ Mon–Fri 10–12, 2–4
✦ Inexpensive

Waag
✉ Markt 35–6
☎ 0182/529 996
◷ Apr–Oct Tue, Wed, Fri 1–5, Thu 10–5
✦ Inexpensive

Adrie Moerings Pottenbakkerij & Pijpenmakerij
✉ Peperstraat 76
☎ 0182/512 842
◷ Mon–Fri 9–5, Sat 11–5
✦ Free

EDAM ✪✪

Home of the famous round, yellow-skinned cheese (covered in red wax for export), Edam, 15km north of Amsterdam, lies inland along a canal from the IJsselmeer. Visit the **Edams Museum**, in a 1530s merchant's house with a floating cellar, for a look at the town's history. A cheese-making display at the Kaaswaag (Cheese-Weighing House) and the beautifully decorated Trouwzaal (Wedding Room) in the 1737 Stadhuis (Town Hall) are worth seeing. The tilting 15th-century Speeltoren (Carillon Tower) has a carillon from 1561. You can tour nearby cheese-making farms; leaflets are available from the VVV office.

GOUDA ✪✪

Gouda, renowned for its yellow-skinned, cylindrical cheese and clay pipes, is 37km south of Amsterdam. Its striking 15th-century Gothic **Stadhuis** (Town Hall), has a carillon whose chimes are accompanied by figures representing Count Floris V signing the town's charter in 1272. You can learn the story of Gouda and cheese at the Cheese Exhibition in the **Waag** (Weigh-House), and of Gouda and pipes at the **Adrie Moerings Pottenbakkerij & Pijpenmakerij**. Visit the 16th-century Sint-Janskerk to see its superb stained-glass windows, some dating from the 1550s. There's a popular cheese market on Thursday mornings in the Markt from June until August.

DEN HAAG & SCHEVENINGEN ✪✪✪

The Netherlands' administrative capital, The Hague (63km southwest of Amsterdam), and its seaside resort Scheveningen have reached out and touched each other over the years, and it makes sense to visit them together.

Den Haag makes an interesting comparison with Amsterdam, having almost no canals, and being focused on government, the royal court, diplomacy and its role as seat of the International Court of Justice. There's plenty to see, beginning with the Dutch parliament, the **Binnenhof**, where both chambers of the States General meet and, in its courtyard, the 13th-century **Ridderzaal (Hall of the Knights)**, where the monarch presides over the annual state opening of parliament. You can visit **Paleis Lange Voorhout**, view Huis ten Bosch (home of Queen Beatrix) from its surrounding park and look at Paleis Noordeinde from the street. For Dutch and international art, including masterpieces by Rembrandt, Vermeer and Van Gogh, visit the **Mauritshuis** and **Haags Gemeentemuseum (Hague Municipal Museum)**. For variety there's the **Omniversum** Imax projection theatre; **Madurodam**, a miniature village, with the best of Holland at a scale of 1:25; and **Panorama Mesdag**, a panoramic painting of Scheveningen made in 1880–1.

Compared with Zandvoort (➤ 89), Amsterdam's seaside resort, **Scheveningen** is the height of sophistication. Though it can be a little ragged around the edges, it's well worth the short tram ride from The Hague to visit its superb belle époque beach hotel, the Steigenberger Kurhaus, casino, fancy shops, good seafood and international restaurants, splendid pier and beach. On the last Saturday in May the harbour is the setting for Vlaggetjesdag (Flag Day), when fishing boats compete for the honour of catching the new season's first herring for the Queen.

🛈 Koningin Julianaplein
☎ 0900/340 3505 📧
Jul–Aug Mon–Sat 9–5:30,
Sun 11–5; Sep–Jun
Mon–Sat 9–5:30

Binnenhof/Ridderzaal
✉ Binnenhof 8a
☎ 070/364 6144
🕐 Guided tours Mon–Sat
10–4 (last tour 3:45).
Closed pub hols, special
events 👢 Moderate

Paleis Lange Voorhout
✉ Lange Voorhout 74
☎ 070/362 4061
🕐 Tue–Sun 11–5
👢 Moderate

Mauritshuis
✉ Korte Vijverberg 8
☎ 070/302 3435
🕐 Tue–Sat 10–5, Sun & pub
hols 11–5. Closed 1 Jan,
25 Dec 👢 Expensive

Haags Gemeentemuseum
✉ Stadhouderslaan 41
☎ 070/338 1111
🕐 Tue–Sun and pub hols
11–5 👢 Expensive

Omniversum
✉ President Kennedylaan 5
☎ 0900/666 4837
🕐 Mon 12–7, Tue–Wed
10–7, Thu–Sun and
during hols 10 –9. Closed
1 Jan, 25 Dec
👢 Very expensive

Madurodam
✉ George Maduroplein 1
☎ 070/355 3900
🕐 Jul–Aug daily 9–10;
Sep–late Mar daily 9–6;
late Mar–Jun daily 9–10
👢 Very expensive

Panorama Mesdag
✉ Zeestraat 65
☎ 070/364 4544
🕐 Mon–Sat 10–5, Sun & pub
hols 12–5. Closed 25 Dec
👢 Moderate

*Peering across at
Scheveningen from the
resort's magnificent pier*

The splendours of St Bavo's Church are its marvellous organ (far right), and the ornate spire (right)

 Stationsplein 1 ☎ 0900/616 1600 🕓 Mon–Fri 9:30–5:30, Sat 10–2

Sint-Bavokerk
✉ Oude Groenmarkt 23
☎ 023/532 4399
🕓 Mon–Sat 10–4
♿ Inexpensive

Frans Halsmuseum
✉ Groot Heiligland 62
☎ 023/511 5775
🕓 Tue–Sat 11–5, Sun & pub hols 12–5. Closed 1 Jan, 25 Dec
♿ Moderate

HAARLEM ✪✪✪

Just 20km west of Amsterdam, this city of 150,000 is often considered to be the capital's fair little sister, with almost as much canal-fringed, Golden Age allure and far fewer everyday vexations. Founded in the 10th century, Haarlem was the seat of the medieval Counts of Holland and is today Noord-Holland's provincial capital. Its lowest ebb was a seven-month siege (1572–3) during Holland's revolt against Spain when, despite desperate resistance, the Duke of Alva's troops captured the city and massacred half its 40,000 inhabitants.

Haarlem's Grote Markt is dominated by the 80m-high tower, adorned with gilt spheres, of the late-Gothic **Sint-Bavokerk** (built 1370–1520), also known as the Grote Kerk (Great Church). In the bright and richly ornamented interior is a 1738 Christian Müller organ, with more than 5,000 pipes, that was once played by Mozart and Handel. You can see, still embedded in the wall, a cannonball that flew through a window during the Spanish siege. The painter Frans Hals (c1580–1666), who was born in Antwerp and lived and worked in Haarlem for most of his life, is buried in the choir. In addition to such highly individualistic works as *The Gypsy Girl* and *The Laughing Cavalier*, Hals painted group portraits of the *schutters* (musketeers), local militia companies. You can see eight such works, among others, at the **Frans Hals Museum**, including the lively *Banquet of the Officers of the St Hadrian Militia Company* (1627). The museum is in the former Oudemannenhuis, an old men's hospice from 1608.

HOORN ⊗⊗

This once important seaport is on the IJsselmeer shore, 32km north of the capital. It makes a possible day trip by bike, returning by train. The best place to appreciate Hoorn's maritime past, which has left the town many old sailors' houses and gabled merchants' villas, is at the busy inner harbour, the Binnenhaven, with its 1532 tower, the Hoofdtoren. Visit the **Westfries Museum** in a baroque building dating from 1632 to sample Hoorn's heritage.

LEIDEN ⊗⊗

Rembrandt's birthplace and the Pilgrim Fathers' refuge before they sailed to America, Leiden is a renowned university town, 36km southwest of Amsterdam. In 1594, botanist Carolus Clusius grew the first tulips in Holland at the botanical garden here. Each year, between 1 and 3 October, Leiden celebrates the raising of the 1574 Spanish siege, when the Dutch Navy sailed across flooded fields after the dikes had been broken, and surprised the Spanish at their dinner of stew.

DID YOU KNOW?

In 1616, Willem Schouten was the first seaman to sail round the southern tip of South America, through the Straits of Magellan, and into the Pacific. He named the rocky, storm-swept point of Tierra del Fuego island Kap Hoorn (Cape Horn) after his home town.

🛈 Veemarkt 4 ☎ 0900/403 1055 🕔 Tue–Sat 9:30–5, (Mon 1–5, 6 in summer)

Westfries Museum
✉ Rode Steen 1
☎ 0229/280 028
🕔 Mon–Fri 11–5, Sat 2–5, Sun 12–5 (winter Sat–Sun 2–5). Closed 1 Jan, 30 Apr, 3rd Mon in Aug, 25 Dec

🛈 Stationsweg 2d
☎ 0900/222 2333
🕔 Mon–Fri 11–5:30, Sat 10–4:30

The IJsselmeer's Western Shore

Distance
160km

Time
A day

Start/end point
Amsterdam

Lunch
De Hoofdtoren, Hoorn (► 99)

For centuries the Zuiderzee, a stormy North Sea inlet, presented a clear and present danger to low-lying Amsterdam – so the Dutch got rid of it. In 1932, the 30km-long Afsluitdijk (Enclosing Dike) shut out the sea. In its place is the IJsselmeer, a freshwater lake and a wonderful setting for a drive through historic towns and typical Dutch scenery.

Take the A10 Amsterdam ring road east to junction 114 and follow the signs to the lake at Durgerdam. Stay on the lakeside road, heading north.

A causeway leads to Marken (► 88), which was once an island. Explore the pretty harbourside village on foot. You can also walk 2km to a lighthouse at the island's tip.

Re-cross the causeway and continue north on the lakeside road.

Monnickendam harbour (► 88) is worth visiting, though most people pass through to Volendam (► 88), a fishing village where you can have your picture taken wearing traditional Dutch costume. A brief detour through Edam (► 80) returns you to the lake.

Continue north through Warder and Scharwoude.

Take a tour around Hoorn (► 83), an historic seaport and fishing village.

Hoorn harbour recalls the town's celebrated maritime history

Going east and north along the shore brings you to Enkhuizen.

Visit Enkhuizen's Zuiderzeemuseum by boat. Many fields around the town are awash with tulips in spring.

Continue to Medemblik.

Visit the harbour, the steam train museum and 13th-century Kasteel Radboud (Radboud Castle).

Continue to the Afsluitdijk. Cross over to the Friesland shore or return to Amsterdam on the A7 (E22).

LOOSDRECHTSE PLASSEN

Old peat diggings filled with water form a cluster of lakes, covering more than 2,500 hectares, that have become a popular watersports zone some 20km southeast of Amsterdam. The lakes, some still connected by strips of peaty soil, are surrounded by picturesque villages: Oud-Loosdrecht, Loenen aan de Vecht, and Breukelen, which in the 17th century gave its name to New York's borough of Brooklyn – there's even a tiny Breukelen Bridge over the River Vecht. These once bucolic villages have become busy harbours for pleasure craft and centres for cafés and restaurants, many with waterside terraces.

Fairytale Muiderslot has been beautifully restored inside and out

MUIDEN

The main reason for visiting this IJsselmeer harbour town, 13km east of Amsterdam, handsome though it is, is to see **Muiderslot**, a turreted, moated castle beside the River Vecht. In 1296, Count Gijsbrecht IV van Aemstel imprisoned and murdered Count Floris V of Holland here. More than three centuries later, the poet Pieter Cornelisz Hooft, a castle steward, founded a literary circle called the Muiderkring (Muiden Circle), which included such luminaries as Hugo Grotius, Joost van den Vondel and Maria Tesselschade.

Muiderslot
✉ Herengracht 1
☎ 0294/261 325
🕐 Guided tours Apr–Sep Mon–Fri 10–5, Sat–Sun & pub hols 1–5 (last tour at 4); Nov–Mar Sat–Sun 1–4 (last tour at 3)
💷 Moderate

NAARDEN

This star-shaped, fortified town, 19km east of Amsterdam, was part of a ring of 17th-century defensive works built to protect heavily populated western Holland. Ironically, the town had been sacked earlier by the Spanish. Its Turfpoort (Peat Gateway) Bastion is an appropriate location for the **Nederlands Vestingmuseum (Dutch Fortifications Museum)**, where you can clamber around the walls and view military exhibits, including weaponry and photographs in the casemates.

Nederlands Vestingmuseum
✉ Westwalstraat 6
☎ 035/694 5459
🕐 Easter–Oct Tue–Fri 10:30–5, Sat–Sun & pub hols 12–5; mid-Jun to Aug also Mon 10:30–5; Nov–Easter 12–5; Sat before Christmas to mid-Jan also Sat & pub hols 12–5. Closed 25 & 31 Dec

🚌 Bus 148

OUDERKERK AAN DE AMSTEL

This handsome village on the River Amstel south of Amsterdam was the seat of the 13th-century Count Gijsbrecht II van Aemstel, who founded Amsterdam. Nowadays there's no doubt which community is in the driving seat. Amsterdammers flock to Ouderkerk to relax in its riverside cafés and restaurants, and it's a popular target for easy cycling excursions along the river.

85

Kijkkubussen
- ✉ Overblaak 70
- ☎ 010/414 2285
- 🕐 Jan–Feb Fri–Sun 11–5;
  Mar–Dec daily 11–5
- 🖐 Inexpensive

Kunsthal
- ✉ Museumpark,
  Westzeedijk 341
- ☎ 010/440 0301
- 🕐 Tue–Sat 10–5, Sun & pub
  hols 11–5. Closed 1 Jan,
  30 Apr, 25 Dec
- 🖐 Moderate

Museum Boijmans Van Beuningen
- ✉ Museumpark 18–20
- ☎ 010/441 9400
- 🕐 See Kunsthal above
- 🖐 Moderate

Above: *cube houses overlooking Oude Haven*

ROTTERDAM ✪✪

Rotterdam, birthplace of the humanist Desiderius Erasmus (1466–1536), began developing as a harbour at the end of the 14th century alongside the foreport of Delft (➤ 79), though it was not until 1886 that it swallowed up Delfshaven. 'Rotterdammers,' say the Dutch, 'are born with their sleeves already rolled up.' That helps explain the speed with which they rebuilt their city, 60km southwest of Amsterdam, which was almost totally destroyed during World War II, and made it the world's most important harbour. The authorities decided in 1945 not to rebuild the devastated city along the old lines, launching instead a bold, controversial and ongoing experiment to create a city of the future. Rotterdam has had all the latest trends in architecture and town planning showered on it and shows no sign of wearying in the quest for modernity. If you like modern architecture, visit the **Kijkkubussen**, one of a group of upended cube-shaped houses on concrete stalks; an apartment tower-block in the shape of a pencil; and an apartment block whose shape has earned it the nickname 'Paper-Clip'.

Grouped conveniently in the Museumpark are the **Kunsthal (Art Hall)**, which mounts art and design exhibitions; **Museum Boijmans Van Beuningen**, whose art collection ranges from Old Masters to the day before yesterday; and the Netherlands Architecture Institute, an appropriate asset for such an architecture-fixated city, though not all of its displays cover modern schools. Get away from museums at Blijdorp Zoo, soar above the harbour at the 188m-high Euromast tower, and tour it on a Spido harbour tour boat.

At Kinderdijk, 12km east of the city, you have the beautiful sight of 19 windmills together in a cluster. These were in use until 1950 to drain the Alblasserwaard polders and are now a popular tourist attraction.

TEXEL ⊙⊙

Texel island, which lies off the Noord-Holland peninsula 70km northwest of Amsterdam, is reached by a 20-minute car ferry crossing from Den Helder, at the tip of the peninsula. Biggest of Holland's Wadden Islands, Texel has a population of 14,000 that surges in summer when visitors pour in for its beaches, boating, cycling and bird-watching. Around 400 bird species have been spotted, including 100 breeding species. You can observe birds at several nature reserves, tour nature trails through dunes and woods, and get close to nature in general, and the island's seal population in particular, on guided tours.

UTRECHT ⊙⊙

Utrecht traces its history back to Roman times and has many memorials of its medieval role as an ecclesiastical centre. About 34km southeast of Amsterdam, the city has a split personality, divided between its old centre along tree-lined Oudegracht and Nieuwegracht – canals whose former warehouses have been turned into cafés and restaurants – and a modern face focused on the vast Hoog Catherijne shopping mall and Vredenburg entertainment complex. Utrecht is dominated by the 14th-century Gothic **Domtoren**, 112m high, and adjacent **Domkerk** (1254–1517), which stands on the site of a cathedral destroyed by a hurricane in 1647.

Texel's sandy beaches are as much an attraction as the abundant birdlife

🛈 Emmalaan 66, Den Burg
☎ 0222/312 847
◉ Mon–Fri 9–6, Sat 9–5

Car ferry
☎ 0222/369 600
◉ Hourly sailings Mon–Sat 6:35AM–9:35PM, Sun and pub hols 8:35AM to 9:35PM; last return 9:05PM. No reservations

🛈 Vinkenburgstraat 19
☎ 0900/414 1414
◉ Mon–Fri 9–6, Sat 9–5

Domtoren and Domkerk
✉ Domplein
☎ Tower: 030/233 3036, cathedral: 030/231 0403
◉ Cathedral: May–Sep daily 10–5; Oct–Apr Mon–Fri 10–4, Sat 11–3:30, Sun 2–4
🏛 Tower: moderate, cathedral: free

87

VOLENDAM AND MARKEN ✪✪✪

These two IJsselmeer resorts, 18km and 16km northeast of Amsterdam respectively, are popular with day-trippers by car, bus, bike and guided tour. Long-time rivals, they face each other across just 3km of water, presenting different faces.

Volendam, on the mainland, is Catholic, rambunctious and open; Marken, a former island connected to the mainland by causeway in 1957, is Calvinist, tranquil and insular. In each, some local people can occasionally be seen wearing traditional costume; you're not guaranteed to see this, but you might. You can easily combine the two resorts in one trip, thereby having a chance to compare and contrast.

Volendam's focus is a long, dike-top street along the harbour, lined with souvenir shops, cafés, restaurants and fish-stalls – try the smoked IJsselmeer *paling* (eel), a speciality. Marken has a harbour too, though a smaller one, lined with green-painted wooden houses on stilts, some of which you can visit; others have been turned into cafés. There are tiny hamlets scattered across the former island's polders, and a lighthouse on the shore. From mid-March to October, a tour boat connects the two resorts, sailing from half-hourly to hourly on a half-hour crossing.

The popular face of Dutch tourism on show in Volendam

Between the two resorts – neutral territory, if you like – lies **Monnickendam**, which has its own busy harbour lined with cafés and restaurants, and which makes less fuss than its neighbours over its status as a tourist attraction.

DE ZAANSE SCHANS ✪✪

This living village and museum, 13km northwest of Amsterdam, offers a glimpse of Dutch life in times past.

Zaanse Schans – bringing the past to life

Set up in 1960 with relocated, green-painted Zaanstreek houses and five windmills, it's almost kitsch, but not quite, thanks to a scenic setting on the River Zaan and the intrinsic interest of the trades it preserves. You can shop at an 18th-century grocery store, and visit a traditional clog-maker, a cheese-maker, pewter workshop, bakery museum, clock museum, working windmills making oil, paint and classic Zaanse mustard, and a sawmill.

ZANDVOORT ✪✪✪

Amsterdam's seaside resort, 25km west of the city, is brash and brassy when it claims its place in the sun every summer (even when there is no sun), and sinks into winter melancholy come the middle of October. Whatever the season or weather, Amsterdammers like nothing better than taking the train here, walking up and down on the beach for an hour or two taking in the atmosphere, then retiring to a café. Zandvoort's long stretch of smooth sand is lined in summer with 40 café-restaurants. You can feel overdressed here wearing only a bikini bottom or swimshorts, particularly at the nudist and gay sections of the beach. Windsurfers are well catered for, and swimming is safe, though the North Sea is generally far from warm.

Away from the beach, splash out in a different way at **Holland Casino Zandvoort**, or catch a motor or motor-cycle race at Circuit Park Zandvoort. For a more leisurely experience, tour the Kennemerduinen National Park's extensive dunes.

ℹ Schoolplein 1 ☎ 023/571 7947 🕐 Apr to mid-Jul & mid-Aug to Sep Mon–Sat 9–5; mid-Jul to mid-Aug Mon–Sat 9–7; Oct–Mar Mon–Sat 10–12:30, 1:30–4:30

Holland Casino Zandvoort
✉ Badhuisplein 7
☎ 023/574 0574
🕐 Daily 1:30PM–2AM
💰 Moderate (passport and 'correct' attire needed)

On the beach at Zandvoort

The North Sea Coast

Distance
145km

Time
A day

Start/end point
Amsterdam

Lunch
De Pêcherie Haarlem aan Zee
(➤ 99)

VVV Castricum
✉ Dorpsstraat 62
☎ 0251/652 009
🕐 Mon 12–5, Tue–Fri
9:30–5, Sat 9:30–2

The coast west of Amsterdam plays host to a constellation of beach resorts, each with its own distinct character. Driving between them and soaking up bracing sea air makes a nice change from wall-to-wall canals and polders.

Take the A8 northwest from Amsterdam to its end, then via a dogleg on the N246 and N203, to the A9 and continue north to Alkmaar. Change to the N9 for Bergen, then west to Bergen aan Zee.

Visit the beach, its dunes, and the Zee Aquarium.

Go south on the coast road through the Duinreservaat (Dune Reserve) to Egmond, then west to Egmond aan Zee.

The resort has a superb beach, a lighthouse and walking trails through the dunes.

Go south to Castricum, then west through the Noordhollands–Castricum Duinreservaat to Castricum aan Zee.

Dune trails, for which you need a pass from VVV Castricum, are particularly good here.

Stop for a walk through the dune landscape at Kennemerduinen

Go south to Beverwijk, then west to Wijk aan Zee.

Near the mouth of the Noordzeekanaal, this resort is too close for comfort to industrial IJmuiden, but its forested dunes zone is attractive.

Go south under the Noordzeekanaal, past IJmuiden, to Haarlem. Take the N208 to Bloemendaal aan Zee.

This little resort adjoins Zandvoort (➤ 89), Amsterdam's main seaside resort. The Kennemerduinen National Park behind the seafront is a great place for hiking.

Return to Amsterdam on the A5/N5 via Haarlem.

Where To...

Acquiring a taste for Holland, at a baker's (above) and a kebab stand (right)

Amsterdam

Price Guide

Approximate price per person for a three-course meal, without drinks, but including value-added tax (BTW) and 15 per cent service charge:

€ = under €25
€€ = €25–€50
€€€ = over €50

In most restaurants you pay substantially less by ordering the *dagschotel* (dish of the day) or *dagmenu* (menu of the day); some also offer a tourist menu, either in addition to the *dagmenu* or instead of it. Reservations are advised for expensive restaurants. Some others listed here in lower price categories also need to be reserved; because they are so popular they almost never have a free table or they don't have many tables in the first place (or both). In any case it is usually a good idea to phone and check on seat availability. In keeping with Amsterdam's laid-back style, casual dress is acceptable even in the most expensive restaurants – though smart-but-casual will go down better at high-end establishments.

NOTE: All bus/tram numbers relate to trams, unless otherwise stated

Akbar (€€)

Akbar's consistently good curries, tandoori and other dishes don't let Indian cuisine down in this area of abundant but unexceptional international restaurants.

✉ **Korte Leisedwarsstraat 15** ☎ **624 2211** 🕐 **Daily, dinner** 🚊 **1, 2, 5, 6, 7, 10**

Al's Plaice (€)

Never mind the painful pun, Al's traditional British fish 'n' chips are prepared by loving hands, for takeaway or sit-down dining.

✉ **Nieuwendijk 10** ☎ **427 4192** 🕐 **Mon 5PM–10PM, Wed–Sun noon–10PM** 🚊 **1, 2, 5, 6, 13, 17**

Amsterdam (€€)

A handsomely renovated 19th-century water-pumping station is the scene for a cool restaurant, whose menu is a deluge of continental dishes.

✉ **Watertorenplein 6** ☎ **682 2666** 🕐 **Daily 11:30AM–1AM** 🚊 **10**

Asian Caribbean (€–€€)

Big, plant-strewn and bewildering, with cuisine from different Asian countries and Caribbean islands – plus an Argentinian steak house.

✉ **Warmoesstraat 170** ☎ **627 1545** 🕐 **Daily dinner** 🚊 **4, 9, 14, 16, 24, 25**

De Belhamel (€€)

Art nouveau décor and classical music set the tone for polished continental cuisine, and game in season, in an intimate setting with a superb canal view.

✉ **Brouwersgracht 60** ☎ **622 1095** 🕐 **Daily dinner** 🚊 **1, 2, 5, 6, 13, 17**

Bolhoed (€–€€)

Two candlelit canalside rooms enlivened with ethnic art, and hard to beat for the adventurous vegetarian recipes prepared and served with light-hearted panache.

✉ **Prinsengracht 60–62** ☎ **626 1803** 🕐 **Daily noon–11 (Sat 11–11AM)** 🚊 **6, 13, 14, 17**

Bordewijk (€€–€€€)

Deft Mediterranean and Asian culinary touches combine with minimalist décor, adding a modern slant to French dining at this well regarded and popular Jordaan restaurant.

✉ **Noordermarkt 7** ☎ **624 3899** 🕐 **Tue–Sun dinner** 🚊 **1, 2, 5, 6, 13, 17**

De Brakke Grond (€–€€)

Flemish Cultural Centre's darkly atmospheric restaurant, serving bountiful portions of Belgian food, including *waterzooï* (chicken or fish stew) and *paling* (eel), along with better-known steak-frites and mussels. You can wash them down with great beers.

✉ **Nes 43** ☎ **626 0044** 🕐 **Tue–Sat noon–11** 🚊 **4, 9, 14, 16, 24, 25**

Brasserie De Poort (€€)

Wooden beams and Delft blue tiles in an 1870 tavern are the backdrop for fine Dutch dining. Every thousandth steak served (they are individually numbered) comes with a free bottle of wine.

✉ **Hotel Die Port van Cleve, Nieuwezijds Voorburgwal 176–180** ☎ **624 0047** 🕐 **Mon–Fri 7AM–10:30AM and 6–10:30PM, Sat–Sun 6–10:30AM and noon–10:30PM** 🚊 **1, 2, 5, 13, 14, 17**

Brasserie Schiller (€€)

Restored, century-old *jugendstil* monument, rich in wood-panelling and etched and stained glass, serving classic Dutch and international cuisine.

✉ **Hotel Schiller, Rembrandtplein 26–36** ☎ **554 0700** 🕐 Daily 7AM–11PM
🚊 **4, 9, 14**

Breitner (€€)

Carefully prepared French dishes in a light and airy setting with a fine view over the Amstel.

✉ **Amstel 212** ☎ **627 7879**
🕐 **Daily 5PM–midnight**
🚊 **4, 9, 14**

Café Américain (€€)

Popularity with tourists has slightly dimmed the modish cachet of this resplendent art deco café, but the fancy continental cuisine remains effective.

✉ **American Hotel, Leidsekade 97** ☎ **556 3232** 🕐 Daily 10:30AM–midnight 🚊 **1, 2, 5, 6, 7, 10**

Café Roux (€€)

French cuisine in an elegant art nouveau setting that used to be the old town hall's canteen. A Karel Appel mural, *Inquisitive Children* (1949), is a proud fixture.

✉ **Grand Hotel, Oudezijds Voorburgwal 197** ☎ **555 3560**
🕐 **Daily noon–6** 🚊 **4, 9, 14, 16, 24, 25**

Christophe (€€€)

Chef Jean Christophe combines French sensibility with a dash of American seasoning to good effect in his chic canalside restaurant.

✉ **Leliegracht 46** ☎ **625 0807**
🕐 **Dinner only Tue–Sat**
🚊 **13, 14, 17**

Duende (€)

Dark, bustling *tapas* café, popular with Spanish expats, with a large choice of *tapas* – hot and cold snacks.

✉ **Lindengracht 62** ☎ **420 6692** 🕐 Daily 5PM–1AM
🚊 **1, 2, 5, 6, 13, 17**

Espresso Corner Baton (€)

Good for a quick, light lunch, this bustling place serves salads, sandwiches, quiches and more. In summer a large pavement terrace allows you to enjoy the canalside ambience.

✉ **Herengracht 82** ☎ **624 8195** 🕐 Mon–Fri 8–6, Sat–Sun 9–6 🚊 **1, 2, 5, 6, 13, 17**

Excelsior (€€€)

Haunt of celebrities and an occasional royal, this superior restaurant beside the Amstel matches top-flight continental cuisine with plush good looks. Consider the fixed-price menus for slightly more affordable dining. Unusually for Amsterdam, but understandably, formal attire is required.

✉ **Hôtel de l'Europe, Nieuwe Doelenstraat 2–8** ☎ **531 1777** 🕐 Daily 7–11, 12:30–2:30 (except Sat), 7–10:30 🚊 **4, 9, 14, 24, 25**

De Falafel Koning (€)

You won't find better falafel than at this simple snack bar opposite the Tuschinski cinema.

✉ **Regulierssteeg 2** ☎ **421 1423** 🕐 Daily 10AM –1AM
🚊 **4, 9, 14**

Gare de l'Est (€€)

Moody, former working-class coffee-house, enhanced by a conservatory, serving a set, daily-changing Mediterranean menu, with the emphasis on French dishes.

✉ **Cruquiusweg 9** ☎ **463 0620** 🕐 Daily 6PM–1 or 2AM
🚌 **Bus 39, 59**

Gary's Muffins and Bagels (€)

Enter a world of bagels, muffins and cheesecake at this breezy American snack

Where to Eat

If you are on a budget or are set on a truly Dutch experience, try an *eetcafé*. In these café-restaurants the food runs the gamut from traditional Dutch, to modern, stylish, even experimental cooking, though generally not in the same place, and usually for significantly less than you pay in a full-blown restaurant.

'Coffee shops' are not there to sell coffee – although their coffee is often surprisingly good – but legally tolerated soft drugs. You buy coffee in a café and occasionally in a *koffiehuis*. Your nose will quickly tell you the difference if it catches a whiff of the bitter-smelling fug that passes for an atmosphere in a 'coffee shop'.

---

bar. You can choose from eight different kinds of bagel, and 20 different toppings.

✉ **Reguliersdwarsstraat 53**
☎ **420 2406** 🕓 **Daily noon–3 or 4AM** 🚊 4, 9, 14, 16, 24, 25

Girassol (€)

The oldest and best Portuguese restaurant in town, with a menu that covers the mainland and includes dishes from Madeira and the Azores.

✉ **Weesperzijde 135**
☎ **692 3471** 🕓 **Daily dinner** 🚊 6, 7, 10

Golden Temple (€–€€)

Vegetarian food finds its rightful place here in a heavenly setting – if not for the minimalist décor, then for the absence of cigarette smoke. Indian, Arab and Mexican dishes form the unlikely, yet successful mix on offer.

✉ **Utrechtsestraat 125** ☎ **626 1199** 🕓 **Daily 5–10** 🚊 4

Greenwoods (€)

Homey English tea room, serving home-made scones, with jam and clotted cream, chocolate cake and lemon meringue pie.

✉ **Singel 103** ☎ **623 7071**
🕓 **Daily 9:30–7** 🚊 1, 2, 5, 6, 13, 17

Haesje Claes (€–€€)

Eight wood-beamed dining rooms in a house from 1520, serving traditional Dutch cuisine with a 'from canapés to caviar' ethos.

✉ **Spuistraat 273–5** ☎ **624 9998** 🕓 **Daily noon–midnight** 🚊 1, 2, 5

Hemelse Modder (€€)

Chocoholics will appreciate the chocolate mousse that gives 'Heavenly Mud' its name. But first sample a vegetarian main course.

✉ **Oude Waal 9–11** ☎ **624 3203** 🕓 **Dinner only Tue–Sun** 🚇 **Nieuwmarkt**

De Jaren (€–€€)

Trendy grand café in a vast, remodelled bank, serving drinks and snacks downstairs and Dutch and continental food upstairs. The Amstel waterfront terraces are a big draw.

✉ **Nieuwe Doelenstraat 20–22**
☎ **625 5771** 🕓 **Sun–Thu 10AM–1AM, Fri–Sat 10AM–2AM**
🚊 4, 9, 14, 16, 24, 25

Kantjil en de Tijger (€€)

'Antelope and the Tiger' spurns the colonial look and serves spicy Javanese food in a cool, modern setting.

✉ **Spuistraat 291–3** ☎ **620 0994** 🕓 **Daily dinner** 🚊 1, 2, 5

De Kas (€€)

This out-of-the-way eatery in a 1926 greenhouse is currently *the* place for trendy locals. The international dishes with a Mediterranean slant are from a couple of variations on a 3-course, daily-changing fixed menu.

✉ **Kamerlingh Onneslaan 3**
☎ **462 4562** 🕓 **Mon–Fri 12–3, 6:30–10, Sat 6:30–10** 🚊 9

't Klein Kalfje (€)

Old-fashioned Dutch café-restaurant on the edge of town. It attracts an office-worker crowd in summer for lunch on its sheltered, riverside terrace.

✉ **Amsteldijk 355** ☎ **644 5338** 🕓 **Sun–Fri 10AM–10PM (8PM in winter)** 🚌 **Bus 148**

De Knijp (€€)

Instead of gulping down dinner then dashing off to the Concertgebouw, dine here after the concert on French and Dutch dishes served in a split-level bistro.

✉ **Van Baerlestraat 134**
☎ **671 4248** 🕓 **Mon–Fri noon–3; daily 5:30PM–1:30AM**
🚊 3, 5, 12, 16, 24

Het Land van Walem (€€)

Set aside the latest interior design and an urbane menu,

✉ Keizersgracht 449
☎ 625 3544 ⏰ Sun–Thu
9AM–1AM; Fri–Sat 9AM–2AM
🚊 1, 2, 5

Lovers (€€€)
A candlelit dinner while
cruising on the canals,
watching the city's historic
gables glide past, is almost
guaranteed to be a romantic
experience.
✉ Prins Hendrikkade (at
Centraal Station) ☎ 622 2181
⏰ Apr–Oct daily 7:30PM; Nov–
Mar Wed, Fri, Sat 7:30PM 🚊 1,
2, 4, 5, 6, 9, 13, 16, 17, 24, 25

Luxembourg (€)
Grand café with a power-
user image, where the club
sandwiches are renowned
and the dim sum and other
snacks derive from top city
restaurants.
✉ Spuistraat 22–24 ☎ 620
6264 ⏰ Sun–Fri 9AM–1AM,
Fri–Sat 9AM–2AM 🚊 1, 2, 5

Mangerie de Kersentuin
(€€–€€€)
Informal yet polished, with
dishes from around the
world adapted to mostly
Dutch ingredients,
distinctively prepared.
✉ Bilderberg Garden Hotel,
Dijsselhofplantsoen 7 ☎ 570
5600 ⏰ Mon–Fri lunch,
Mon–Sat dinner 🚊 5, 16, 24

Memories of India (€€)
Delicately flavoured tandoori,
Moghlai and vegetarian
cuisine in a setting that
adopts a restrained version
of Indian décor.
✉ Reguliersdwarsstraat 88
☎ 623 5710 ⏰ Daily dinner
🚊 4, 9, 14

Metz (€)
The panoramic canal views
from this comfortably
English sixth-floor café

distract memorably from
afternoon tea, as does the
attractive 1933 round glass
rooftop designed by Gerrit
Rietveld.
✉ Metz & Co, Keizersgracht
455/Leidsestraat 34–6 ☎ 520
7020 ⏰ Mon 11–6, Tue, Wed,
Fri, Sat 9:30–6, Thu 9:30–9. Sun
12–5 🚊 1, 2, 5

Mokkalie (€€)
One of a handful of Korean
restaurants in the city. It
does a particularly fine
bulgogi (marinated beef
grilled at your table). This is
all served in a plant-strewn
setting to the chirping of
exotic birds.
✉ Utrechtsestraat 42 ☎ 625
9251 ⏰ Dinner only. Closed
Mon 🚊 4

Moko (€€)
Sample a South Seas-cum-
fusion experience in this
trendy eatery that manages
to be designer-chic and
comfy at the same time.
There's DJ music at
weekends, and an outdoor
terrace set back from
Prinsengracht.
✉ Amstelveld 12 ☎ 626 8560
⏰ Daily 11:30am–1am (until
2am on Sat, Sun), Closed Mond
Nov–Apr 🚊 4

Morita-Ya (€)
Traditional Japanese snack
bar that eschews the
hallowed atmosphere of
many Japanese restaurants
in favour of a convivial local
style, and serves great sushi
and sashimi.
✉ Zeedijk 18 ☎ 638 0756
⏰ Dinner Thu–Tue 🚊 1, 2, 4,
5, 9, 13, 16, 17, 24, 25

Pacifico (€€)
Authentic Mexican food in
a cramped and smoky
bodega, with a wide-ranging
menu, including vegetarian
dishes.
✉ Warmoesstraat 31 ☎ 624
2911 ⏰ Daily dinner 🚊 1, 2,
4, 5, 9, 13, 16, 17, 24, 25

Misconstrued Spice
When the Dutch began
colonising the Spice
Islands of the East Indies
during the 17th century,
they got more than
seasoning out of them.
They developed a taste for
the exotic local cuisine
that survived Indonesian
independence in 1949 and
has bequeathed Holland
an abundance of
Indonesian restaurants.
Most of them serve
rijsttafel (▶ 53). A myth
has grown up around this
'typically Indonesian' meal
that isn't. Dutch colonists
invented it, constantly
adding more dishes to a
basic Indonesian meal until
the table groaned under
their weight. *Rijsttafel*
makes a great introduction
to this national cuisine,
and a great dining
experience – so much so
that some Chinese, Thai,
Vietnamese and Japanese
restaurants have adopted
the approach.

Al Fresco Dining

Amsterdammers are fresh-air fanatics. At the first hint of good weather, restaurants and cafés with outdoor terraces fill up instantly, while those without are left on the vine. The city is a terrace-hound's dream. Hundreds spread out tables and chairs in squares such as Leidseplein and Rembrandtplein, along the canals and the River Amstel, beside the harbour, in parks and back gardens, on rooftops, quiet side-streets and busy main streets – anywhere, in fact, where there's space and the prospect of catching some sun.

Pasta e Basta (€€)

Very popular partly because of its chi-chi Italian food and partly because the staff are liable to burst into live opera at every opportunity.

✉ Nieuwe Spiegelstraat 8 ☎ 422 2229 🕔 Daily 6PM–midnight 🚊 16, 24, 25

De Prins (€–€€)

Bustling brown café (➤ 114) with an above-average, small busy restaurant, and with a daily changing menu of Dutch and vaguely French dishes chalked on black-boards.

✉ Prinsengracht 124 ☎ 624 9382 🕔 Daily 10AM–midnight 🚊 6, 13, 14, 17

La Rive (€€€)

High-end French cuisine with a light, modern touch delivered in a plush and formal two-Michelin-star *salle* overlooking the Amstel.

✉ Amstel InterContinental Hotel, Professor Tulpplein 1 ☎ 622 6060 🕔 Mon–Fri lunch, Mon–Sat dinner. Closed Sat–Sun lunch, Sun dinner 🚊 6, 7, 10

Rose's Cantina (€–€€)

Noisy place whose Tex-Mex food in a vaguely Mexican setting is unexceptional, yet whose camaraderie – and great margaritas – mean it's hard to get a table.

✉ Reguliersdwarsstraat 38–40 ☎ 625 9797 🕔 Daily dinner 🚊 1, 2, 5

Royal Café De Kroon (€€)

Turn-of-the-century grand café that closed during the 1960s and reopened to general acclaim during the 1990s. You order from an eclectic world menu and can sit in the almost harshly modern designer interior or on an enclosed balcony overlooking the square.

✉ Rembrandtplein 17 ☎ 625 2011 🕔 Daily 10AM–1AM (Fri–Sat 2AM) 🚊 4, 9, 14, 20

La Ruche (€)

Take the weight off shopping-weary feet over coffee and apple-pie with fresh cream in this department store café overlooking the Dam.

✉ De Bijenkorf, Dam 1 ☎ 621 8080 🕔 Mon–Wed, Sat 9:30–6, Thu 9:30–9, Sun noon–6 🚊 4, 9, 14, 16, 24, 25

Rum Runners (€–€€)

Caribbean food and cocktails are served in a tropical setting in the Westerkerk's former coach house beside the Anne Frankhuis.

✉ Prinsengracht 277 ☎ 627 4079 🕔 Mon–Thu 2PM–1AM, Fri–Sun 2PM–2AM 🚊 6, 13, 14, 17

Sal Meijer's (€)

For the finest kosher snacks and sandwiches in town, head for Amsterdam South and this focal point of the city's Jewish community. Or call and ask about a delivery to your hotel.

✉ Scheldestraat 45 ☎ 673 1313 🕔 Sun–Fri 10–7:30 🚊 25

Sea Palace (€€)

It might not have the best Chinese food in town, but eating aboard a pagoda-style floating restaurant in the harbour, modelled on Hong Kong's famous Jumbo restaurant, adds romance to the experience.

✉ Oosterdokskade 8 ☎ 626 4777 🕔 Daily noon–midnight 🚊 1, 2, 4, 5, 6, 9, 13, 16, 17, 24, 25

Shibli (€€€)

Sit on a sofa inside a tent amid Bedouin ornaments and rugs, dining on a sophisticated Arab banquet, and finish with a puff of apple-and-honey tobacco from a *hookah* (water-pipe).

✉ Hotel Krasnapolsky, Dam 9 ☎ 330 8082 🕔 Thu–Sun dinner 🚊 4, 9, 14, 16, 24, 25

De Silveren Spiegel (€€)

The 'Silver Mirror', in twin step-gabled houses dating from 1614, reflects good taste with sophisticated traditional Dutch cuisine enhanced by a continental tang.

✉ Kattengat 4–6 ☎ 624 6589 🕘 Mon–Sat dinner 🚊 1, 2, 5, 13, 17

Tempo Doeloe (€€)

Although served on fine china atop linen tablecloths, a few of the *rijsttafel* dishes here can be as fiery as Krakatoa erupting. Don't let that put you off sampling some of the city's best Indonesian dining.

✉ Utrechtsestraat 75 ☎ 625 6718 🕘 Daily dinner 🚊 4

Traiterie Grekas (€€)

If you can get a seat at this tiny, authentic Greek eatery, most of which's business comes from its takeaway service, grab it. Salad dishes and main courses are on display behind glass; you point to what you want and it's brought to your table.

✉ Singel 311 ☎ 620 3590 🕘 Tue–Fri and Sun 4PM–9:30PM, Sat 1PM–9:30PM 🚊 1, 2,5

Vertigo (€€)

Brown café setting, where menu dishes occasionally reflect themes from the adjacent Film Museum – a Japanese film season might be complemented by sushi and sashimi. The terrace in the park is one of the best in town.

✉ Vondelpark 3 ☎ 612 3021 🕘 Daily 11AM (from 10 during Jul–Aug)–1AM 🚊 1, 2, 3, 5, 6, 12

D'Vijff Vlieghen (€€)

With seven individually decorated dining-rooms, the 'Five Flies' flits through a variety of Old Dutch interior styles while focusing culinary attention on light, sophisticated New Dutch cooking.

✉ Spuistraat 294–302 ☎ 624 8369 🕘 Daily dinner 🚊 1, 2, 5

In de Waag (€€)

The ground floor of an old city gate and weigh house (➤ 73) has been transformed into a restaurant with a medieval look – you dine at long, candlelit benches – and totally modern taste from a wide range of international dishes.

✉ Nieuwmarkt 4 ☎ 422 7772 🕘 Daily 10AM–1AM 🚇 Nieuwmarkt

Wildschut (€–€€)

A chic, art deco bistro that attracts an arts and media crowd and serves up international dishes from BLTs through pasta to 'surf and turf'. When the sun shines, the curving pavement terrace is one of the best in town.

✉ Roelof Hartplein 1–3 ☎ 676 8220 🕘 Mon–Fri 9AM–1AM, Sat 10:30AM–1AM, Sun 9:30AM–midnight 🚊 3, 5, 12, 24

Wilhelmina-Dok (€€)

Dining at this waterside place in Amsterdam-Noord involves a 5-minute 'voyage' by ferry across the IJ channel behind Centraal Station. Nautical setting, good continental food and great waterway views.

✉ Nordwal 1 ☎ 632 3701 🕘 Mon–Fri noon–midnight, Sat–Sun noon–1AM 🚢 IJ Ferry to IJplein

Le Zinc...et les Dames (€€)

Hearty portions of provincial French cuisine in a wood-beamed canalside warehouse converted to a fashionably homey restaurant.

✉ Prinsengracht 999 ☎ 622 9044 🕘 Tue–Sat dinner only 🚊 4

Vegetarians

The Dutch have traditionally been meat-and-veg people. More often now the meat is left out and the veg dressed up in a variety of internationally minded ways. You will find no shortage of purely vegetarian eateries, many with a style that leaves the scrubbed-pine-and-sandals image light years behind; and many more mixed restaurants now have a special place for vegetarians on their menu. Full vegetarian restaurants listed here are Bolhoed (➤ 92) and Golden Temple (➤ 94).

Raw Fish

If this is your thing there's nowhere better to try a traditional Dutch raw herring that at Van Altena (€) in Stadhouderskade on the corner of Jan Luijkenstraat beside the Rijksmuseum. You can sample other fishy delights, too, and accompany them with a glass of fine wine (☎ 676 9136 🕘 Tue– Sun 11–7 🚊 6, 7, 10).

Excursions from the City

Dutch Taste

Look out for soup tureen icons in the red, white and blue colours of the Dutch flag, that identify the members of the Neerlands Dis (Netherlands Dish) association. Its restaurants dedicate themselves to preparing the best Dutch produce from land and sea and serving up the results in traditional fashion and to a high standard of quality. There's no better way to go Dutch.

Delft

Spijshuis de Dis (€€)
Steaks are the speciality and Dutch food with a touch of class is the trademark at this traditional restaurant.
✉ Beestenmarkt 36 ☎ 015/213 1782 🕐 Thu–Tue 5PM–9:30PM.

Stads Pannekoekhuys (€)
Traditional pancake house with 90 different kinds of pancake on its roster.
✉ Oude Delft 113–115 ☎ 015/213 0193 🕐 Apr–Sep daily 11–9; Oct–Mar Tue–Sun 11–9

Edam

De Fortuna (€€)
The flower-bedecked canalside terrace and wood-beamed, Old Holland interior are the setting for typically Dutch, with a dash of French, menu dishes.
✉ Spuistraat 3 ☎ 0299/371 671 🕐 Daily 6PM–10PM

Gouda

Mallemolen (€€)
Canalside restaurant with Old Dutch looks and French cuisine – even the cheeses, in this most emblematic of Dutch cheese towns, are of French provenance.
✉ Oosthaven 72 ☎ 0182/515 430 🕐 Tue–Fri noon–2PM and 5PM–midnight, Sat–Sun 5PM–midnight

Den Haag & Scheveningen

Ducdalf (€€)
Nautical style in a fishing harbour setting. It doesn't make fish a fetish, but provides a large variety with good taste. There are meat dishes, too.
✉ Dr Lelykade 5, Scheveningen ☎ 070/355 7692 🕐 Daily noon–10

't Goude Hooft (€€)
Quaint 17th-century looks disguise the effects of a 20th-century fire. Rebuilt in the old style, with wooden beams and brass chandeliers, it's a great place for everything from a beer to a full-scale Dutch meal, in the handsome interior or on a terrace overlooking the square.
✉ Groenmarkt 13, The Hague ☎ 070/346 9713 🕐 Mon–Sat 10AM–midnight, Sun 11AM–midnight

Greve (€)
A brightly lit café and a cosy restaurant are the two contrasting faces of this fashionable place, with an international menu that emphasises Mediterranean dishes.
✉ Torenstraat 138, The Hague ☎ 070/360 3919 🕐 Cafe: daily 10AM–1AM; restaurant: Sun–Wed 6PM–10PM, Thu–Sat 6PM–11PM

Kandinsky (€€–€€€)
A fine restaurant with a great beachside location and sea view. Serves superior French and Mediterranean cuisine.
✉ Steigenberger Kurhaus Hotel, Gevers Deynootplein 30, Scheveningen ☎ 070/416 2636 🕐 Mon–Fri 12–10 (no lunch Jul–Aug), 6–10:30, Sat 6–10:30

Haarlem

Jacobus Pieck (€–€€)
Stylish café-restaurant with a shady garden terrace and an eclectic menu that runs from snack-type fare at lunchtime to nicely done Dutch and international dishes for dinner.
✉ Warmoesstraat 18 ☎ 023/532 6144 🕐 Mon–Sat 10AM–11PM, Sun noon–11PM

De Pêcherie Haarlem aan Zee (€€)

Bright and breezy seafood specialist, kitted out with beach props and marine fittings, and a menu of well-prepared fish dishes.

✉ Oude Groenmarkt 10 ☎ 023/531 4848 🕓 Mon–Sat noon–midnight, Sun 5PM–midnight

Hoorn

De Hoofdtoren (€–€€)

A stonebuilt harbourside defence tower from 1532 is an atmospheric setting for modest Dutch fare such as steaks and grilled fish.

✉ Hoofd 2 ☎ 0229/215 487 🕓 Daily 10–10

Leiden

Stadscafé Van der Werff (€)

This busy café-restaurant serves a range of European dishes in a characterful 1930s mansion.

✉ Steenstraat 2 ☎ 071/513 0335 🕓 Daily 10:30–10

Rotterdam

Brasserie Henkes (€€)

A former gin distillery with a waterfront terrace and an old-fashioned interior, serving Dutch and European dishes.

✉ Voorhaven 17 ☎ 010/425 5596 🕓 Daily 11:30AM–midnight (kitchen closes at 10)

Old Dutch (€€)

Alongside a raft of tasty, traditional dishes, some equally good French ones add a dash of sophistication.

✉ Rochussenstraat 20 ☎ 010/436 0344 🕓 Mon–Fri noon–midnight, Sat 6PM–midnight

Texel

Hostellerie Keijser (€€)

Texel specialities such as the lamb that grazes on the island's salty grass, and fish, in a homey setting.

✉ Herenstraat 34, Den Hoorn ☎ 0222/319 623 🕓 Daily noon–10

Utrecht

Stadskasteel Oudaen (€€–€€€)

Restaurant and café in a 14th-century canalside house. The menu leans towards Dutch and European dishes, often with a medieval slant.

✉ Oudegracht 99 ☎ 030/231 1864 🕓 Café: daily 10AM–2AM; restaurant: Mon–Sat 5:30PM–10PM

Volendam & Marken

Spaander (€€)

Old Dutch dining room that looks like a sailing ship interior, serving Dutch meals with the stress on seafood.

✉ Spaander Hotel, Haven 15–19, Volendam ☎ 0299/363595 🕓 Daily 10–10

De Taanderij (€)

French and vegetarian dishes predominate at this refined interpretation of a traditional Dutch *eethuis*. The coffee and apple-pie with cream is state of the art.

✉ Havenbuurt 1, Marken ☎ 0299/602 206 🕓 Apr–Sep daily 10–10; Oct–Mar Tue–Sun 10–10, Sun 6–10

Zaanse Schans

De Hoop op d' Swarte Walvis (€€€)

Epicurean bliss on the banks of the River Zaan, with mainly French and Dutch dishes served indoors or on a riverside terrace.

✉ Kalverringdijk 15 ☎ 075/616 5629 🕓 Mon–Sat noon–2:30, 6–10

Zandvoort

't Familie Restaurant (€)

Goes a little beyond standard fare, with French-influenced meat courses and stewed eel for the determinedly Dutch, in a breezy family restaurant.

✉ Kerkstraat 27 ☎ 023/571 2537 🕓 Daily noon–10

Rijsttafel Wars

Amsterdam considers itself Holland's market leader in everything, and it is particularly confident that its line-up of Indonesian restaurants is the best in the land. So too, does The Hague, ably supported by its seaside resort, Scheveningen. Both Amsterdam and The Hague point to their extensive ethnic Indonesian communities and to the authentic nature of their local champions in the genre. It's all a matter of taste, of course, and neither city suffers from a lack of choice. If you want an informed part in the debate, be prepared to undertake extensive, but rewarding, research.

Amsterdam

Hotel Rates

Rates are for double rooms; in some hotels you get a reduction for single occupancy of a double. A 5 per cent city tax is added to rates in 4- and 5-star hotels. Most hotels accept credit cards, though some budget hotels may ask you not to use them.

In general, only expensive hotels charge extra for breakfast. 'Breakfast included' can mean an excellent full, buffet, Continental or Dutch breakfast; some budget hotels interpret 'Dutch' breakfast to mean a cup of miserable coffee, an ultra-hard-boiled egg, and a couple of thin, curly slices of cheese and ham.

€ = under €100
€€ = €100–€250
€€€ = over €250

NOTE: All bus/tram numbers relate to trams, unless otherwise stated

Acacia (€)

Small Jordaan hotel owned by an enthusiastic couple who keep things comfortable and friendly. Also rooms on a nearby pair of houseboats.
✉ Lindengracht 251 ☎ 622 1460; fax 638 0748;
www.hotelacacia.nl 🚊 3, 10

De Admiraal (€)

A 17th-century spice warehouse with a nautical style makes a romantic setting for a canalside hotel. The rooms don't quite match the cosy public spaces.
✉ Herengracht 563
☎ 626 2150; fax 623 4625
🚊 4, 9, 14

American (€€€)

Fanciful mix of Venetian gothic and art nouveau distinguishes a hotel that's maybe a little too aware of its own good looks. The art deco Café Américain is a city landmark (➤ 93).
✉ Leidsekade 97 ☎ 556 3000; fax 556 3001; www.amsterdam-american.crowneplaza.com
🚊 1, 2, 5, 6, 7, 10

Amstel Botel (€)

Floating hotel that fits right in with Amsterdam's watery origins. Outboard rooms afford a view of the old harbour area. Facilities are modern and comfortable.
✉ Oosterdokskade 2–4
☎ 626 4247; fax 639 1952;
www.amstelbotel.com
🚇 Centraal Station 🚊 1, 2, 4, 6, 5, 9, 13, 16, 17, 24, 25

Amsterdam (€€)

Fully modernised behind its 18th-century façade, on one of the city's liveliest streets. De Roode Leeuw restaurant serves excellent traditional Dutch food.

✉ Damrak 93–94 ☎ 555 0666; fax 620 4716;
www.hotelamsterdam.nl
🚇 Centraal Station 🚊 4, 9, 14, 16, 24, 25

Arena (€€)

A converted 19th-century orphanage hosts a youth-oriented hotel with stylish modern rooms and one of the city's hottest dance clubs, and a café-restaurant with a garden terrace.
✉ 's Gravesandestraat 51 ☎ 663 3021; fax 663 2649;
www.hotelarena.nl 🚊 3, 7, 10

Belga (€)

Backpackers' *pied-à-terre*, with large rooms suitable for multiple occupancy and a friendly, family-owned style that complements a 17th-century building that was designed by Rembrandt's frame-maker.
✉ Hartenstraat 8 ☎ 624 9080; fax 623 6862 🚊 1, 2, 5, 6, 13, 14, 17

Bilderberg Hotel Jan Luyken (€€)

Flawless and personable service in a graceful 19th-century town house with 65 rooms on a quiet street near Vondelpark, Museumplein and P C Hooftstraat's shopping.
✉ Jan Luijkenstraat 54–8
☎ 573 0730; fax 676 3841;
www.janluyken.nl
🚊 2, 5

Die Port van Cleve (€€€)

One-time Heineken brewery turned hotel, restored and renovated, with modern yet comfortable rooms.
✉ Nieuwezijds Voorburgwal 176–80 ☎ 624 4860; fax 622 0240; www.dieportvancleve.com
🚊 1, 2, 5, 6, 13, 17

Estheréa (€€)

Family-owned hotel that's an ideal compromise between modern facilities and traditional Dutch style, with a great location in 17th-century canalside houses, and well-equipped rooms.

✉ **Singel 303–9** ☎ **624 5146; fax 623 9001; www.estherea.nl**
🚊 **1, 2, 5**

De l'Europe (€€€)

Prestigious hotel combining belle epoque architecture with opulent fittings and the most modern amenities, in an superb riverside setting.

✉ **Nieuwe Doelenstraat 2–8** ☎ **531 1777; fax 531 1778; www.leurope.nl** 🚊 **4, 9, 14, 16, 24, 25**

Grand Hotel Krasnapolsky (€€€€)

Built in the 1860s, the 'Kras' has spread through adjacent buildings, and added up-to-the-minute amenities to its venerable core. Highlight is the *belle époque* Wintertuin (Winter Garden) restaurant.

✉ **Dam 9** ☎ **554 8080; fax 622 8607; www.nh-hotels.com**
🚊 **4, 9, 14, 16, 24, 25**

Grand Sofitel Demeure (€€€)

During its 400-plus years, this has been a convent, a gentlemen's residence, Admiralty offices and the town hall. It's now a plush hotel with all amenities.

✉ **Oudezijds Voorburgwal 197** ☎ **555 3111; fax 555 3222; www.thegrand.nl** 🚊 **4, 9, 14, 16, 24, 25**

NH Barbizon Palace (€€€)

Luxury and modern amenities concealed behind the façades of a row of 17th-century houses facing Centraal Station.

✉ **Prins Hendrikkade 59–72** ☎ **556 4564; fax 624 3353; www.nh-hotels.com**
🚉 **Centraal Station** 🚊 **1, 2, 4, 5, 6, 9, 13, 16, 17, 24, 25**

Pulitzer (€€–€€€)

A real prizewinner, spread through two dozen 17th- and 18th-century canal houses with gardens. Facilities among the bare brick and oak beams are generally modern and stylish.

✉ **Prinsengracht 315–331** ☎ **523 5235; fax 627 6753; www.pulitzer.nl**
🚊 **6, 13, 14, 17**

Seven Bridges (€€)

Small and exquisite, with a view of seven bridges, individually styled rooms, lots of antiques, and owners who really do treat their guests like family friends.

✉ **Reguliersgracht 31** ☎ **623 1329 (also fax)** 🚊 **4, 16, 24, 25**

Sint-Nicolaas (€)

If a former factory doesn't sound appealing, rest assured that this rambling place near Centraal Station has a touch of class and comfortable facilities.

✉ **Spuistraat 1a** ☎ **626 1384; fax 623 0979; www.hotel nicolas.nl** 🚉 **Centraal Station** 🚊 **1, 2, 5, 6, 13, 17**

Stayokay Amsterdam Vondelpark (€)

A big new hostel built around an old one in the city's famous park, adding a range of modern options from doubles and family rooms to small dormitories, some of which are women-only.

✉ **Zandpad 5, Vondelpark** ☎ **589 8999; fax 589 8955; www.stayok.com/vondelpark**
🚊 **1, 2, 5, 6, 10**

Van Ostade Bicycle Hotel (€)

Small, well-kept place that hires bicycles and gives maps and advice on how to discover the city's less well-known places by bike.

✉ **Van Ostadestraat 123** ☎ **679 3452; fax 671 5213; www.bicyclehotel.com**
🚊 **3, 12, 24, 25**

Hotel Tips

Two-fifths of Amsterdam's 30,000 hotel beds are in 4- and 5-star properties, which can make things difficult for people wanting mid-range and budget accommodation, particularly at peak times such as during the spring tulip season and summer. It's always best to book ahead.

If you arrive without a reservation, go to one of the VVV tourist offices which can guarantee to find you something, though it may not be in the class or area you prefer. Watch out for hidden pitfalls, such as Golden Age canalhouses with four or five floors, steep, narrow stairways, and no lifts; and tranquil-looking mansions with a late-night café terrace next door.

Excursions from the City

Bijou Properties
Wherever possible, the hotels listed in this section have been chosen for having something more in the way of local character than their name. This has often meant selecting hotels in old buildings, some transformed from their original purpose. There are plenty of alternatives, though, if you just want a straightforward modern hotel with few trimmings or an unpretentious budget hotel with even less.

Edam
De Fortuna (€–€€)
Canalside hotel in the heart of town, with a 17th-century main building, garden and up-to-date amenities.
✉ Spuistraat 3 ☎ 0299/371 671; fax 0299/371 469; www.fortuna-edam.nl

Delft
De Kok (€–€€)
Four connected mansions form this stylish hotel between the railway station and the old centre. Rooms are modern and there's a large garden with a fountain.
✉ Houttuinen 14 ☎ /fax 015/212 2125; www.hoteldekok.nl

Leeuwenbrug (€€)
In two town-centre canalside buildings, with Old Dutch public rooms and plain but modern guest rooms.
✉ Koornmarkt 16 ☎ 015/214 7741; fax 015/215 9759; www.leeuwenbrug.nl

Den Haag & Scheveningen
Astoria (€)
Small, family-owned hotel near the Hollands Spoor railway station. Facilities are minimal but its rooms are comfortable and clean.
✉ Stationsweg 139, The Hague ☎ 070/384 0401; fax 070/354 1653 🚌 11, 12

Des Indes InterContinental (€€€)
Height of elegance, in an 1880s baronial mansion. Its rooms are the last word in comfort and amenities, its dining areas fashionable meeting-places.
✉ Lange Voorhout 54–6, The Hague ☎ 070/361 2345; fax 070/345 1721; www.desindes.com 🚌 1, 3, 7, 8, 9, 12

Mercure Den Haag Central (€€)
Big, ultramodern city-centre hotel that makes up in comfort and efficiency what it may lack in character.
✉ Spui 180, The Hague ☎ 070/363 6700; fax 070/363 9398; www.mercure.com 🚌 1, 8, 9, 10, 16, 17

Parkhotel (€€)
Characterful modern hotel with modestly comfortable rooms, on a quiet, embassy-lined street overlooking Zorgvliet Park.
✉ Molenstraat 53, The Hague ☎ 070/362 4371; fax 070/361 4525; www.parkhoteldenhaag.nl 🚌 7

Steigenberger Kurhaus (€€€)
Palatial national monument on the seafront, with luxuriously appointed rooms and smart restaurants and cafés, including the *belle époque* Kurzaal restaurant and concert hall.
✉ Gevers Deynootplein 30, Scheveningen ☎ 070/416 2636; fax 070/416 2646; www.kurhaus.nl 🚌 1, 9

Leiden
Hotel de Doelen (€)
Elegant, small canalside hotel, incorporating a 15th-century merchant's house and retaining some period character.
✉ Rapenburg 2 ☎ 071/512 0527; fax 071/512 8453; www.dedoelen.com 🚌 43

Rotterdam
Bilderberg Parkhotel (€€)
Ultramodern hotel near Centraal Station, with

plushly furnished and well-equipped rooms and a garden restaurant.

✉ **Westersingel 70**
☎ **010/436 3611; fax 010/436 4212; www.bilderberg.nl** 🚌 **5**

New York (€–€€)

An 11-storey 'skyscraper' built between 1897 and 1898 as the Holland-America Line's headquarters is now a hotel that retains some old office fittings and has modern rooms and great harbour views.

✉ **Koninginnenhoofd 1**
☎ **010/439 0500; fax 010/484 2701; www.hotelnewyork.nl**
🚌 **20**

Texel
Koogerend (€€)

Recently renovated, this attractive, red-roofed hotel in the centre of the island's diminutive capital has modern wings built around a traditional house.

✉ **Koogerstraat 94, Den Burg**
☎ **0222/313301; fax 0222/315902; www.fletcher.nl**

Grand Hotel Opduin (€€)

Modern hotel with large, comfortable rooms and a swimming-pool and sauna, behind the sea-defence dunes on the west coast.

✉ **Ruyslaan 22, De Koog**
☎ **0222/317 445; fax 0222/317 777; www.opduin.nl**

Utrecht
Malie (€–€€)

Though out of the centre, this attractive small hotel in two century-old villas has room décor that matches its genteel surroundings.

✉ **Maliestraat 2/4**
☎ **030/231 6424; fax 030/234 0661; www.maliehotel.nl**
🚌 **4, 11**

Park Plaza Utrecht (€€)

Large, modern chain hotel beside the railway station, convenient for the centre. Well-equipped rooms at a good price.

✉ **Westplein 50** ☎ **030/292-5200; fax 030/292-5199; www.parkplazaww.com**
🚉 **Utrecht Station**

Tulip Inn Utrecht

Turn-of-the-19th-century, city-centre hotel with a high standard of facilities and cosy rooms.

✉ **Janskerkhof 10** ☎ **030/231 3169; fax 030/231 0148; www.nh-hotels.com** 🚌 **2, 3, 11, 12, 22**

Volendam
Spaander (€€)

Animated harbourside hotel that mixes old-fashioned country charm with bright, modernly furnished rooms. The hotel also has a swimming-pool.

✉ **Haven 15–19** ☎ **0299/363 595; fax 0299/369 615; www.bestwestern.nl**

Zandvoort
NH Zandvoort (€€)

Zandvoort's finest hotel offers a good package of amenities, including a beachfront location, swimming-pool, sports facilities and modern rooms, at a moderate price.

✉ **Burgemeester van Alphenstraat 63** ☎ **023/576 0760; fax 023/571 9094; www.nh-hotels.com**

Zuiderbad (€)

Superior family hotel, with a sea view, plainly furnished but well-equipped rooms and a pavement café.

✉ **Boulevard Paulus Loot 5**
☎ **023/571 2613; fax 023/571 3190; www.hotelzuiderbad.nl**

Bed and Breakfast

If you are touring from Amsterdam and don't want to pre-book a hotel, you'll find lots of B&B accommodation in many areas. Either visit the local VVV tourist office, which will have a comprehensive list of establishments in its area and can book for you, or simply choose a place as you pass by. Some have 'B&B' signs, but they are more usually identified by 'room-free' signs in Dutch: '*Kamer Vrij*'; and German: '*Zimmer Frei*'.

Art, Antiques & Books

Shopping Areas

Many art galleries and antiques shops are concentrated in the Spiegelkwartier along Spiegelgracht and Nieuwe Spiegelstraat. Rokin has more galleries and up-market boutiques, and Kalverstraat, Damrak and Leidsestraat are popular shopping streets. On P C Hooftstraat and Van Baerlestraat you find designer shops. The Jordaan and small connecting streets in the northern canal ring are the places for second-hand shops and off-beat little boutiques. There's a cluster of bookshops on Kalverstraat and around Spui. Warmoesstraat and the Red Light District specialise in erotic goods.

Antiques

Amsterdam Antiques Gallery

A group of six dealers under one roof on the city's main antiques street, selling quality paintings, silver, pewter, Delft blue and more.

✉ **Nieuwe Spiegelstraat 134** ☎ **625 3371** 🚊 **6, 7, 10**

Kunst–Antiekcentrum De Looier

Rambling art and antiques market in a collection of old warehouses, with 160-plus dealers selling everything from valuable heirlooms to collectable gewgaws.

✉ **Elandsgracht 109** ☎ **624 9038** 🚊 **7, 10, 17**

Premsela & Hamburger

Dutch royalty gives its seal of approval, and its custom, to this refined setting for antique and contemporary silver and jewellery. Also does repair work.

✉ **Rokin 98** ☎ **624 9688** 🚊 **4, 9, 14, 16, 24, 25**

Art

De Praktijk

Run by a local enthusiast, this gallery in the Jordaan focuses on moderately priced modern Dutch painting and photography.

✉ **Lauriergracht 96** ☎ **422 1727** 🚊 **10, 17**

Jaski Art Gallery

Painting, sculpture, graphic works and ceramics by mainly Cobra artists from 1948–51, including works by later artists.

✉ **Nieuwe Spiegelstraat 27–9** ☎ **620 3939** 🚊 **6, 7, 10**

Books

American Book Center

In addition to its mainstream books, this multi-floor store has strong specialist sections, including gay, erotic, science fiction and fantasy books, as well as second-hand magazines, war-games and sword-and-sorcery games.

✉ **Kalverstraat 185** ☎ **625 5537** 🚊 **4, 9, 14, 16, 24, 25**

Athenaeum Boekhandel

An art nouveau store from 1904 divided into a warren of nooks and crannies for mainly high-brow books in different languages. The attached Athenaeum Nieuwshandel sells international newspapers and magazines.

✉ **Spui 14–16** ☎ **622 6248** 🚊 **1, 2, 5**

De Slegte

The city's largest second-hand bookshop has a vast choice of titles in multiple languages on several floors.

✉ **Kalverstraat 48–52** ☎ **622 5933** 🚊 **4, 9, 14, 16, 24, 25**

Vrolijk Gay and Lesbian Bookstore

Large range of books, primarily in English. Often cheaper than gay sections of mainstream stores.

✉ **Paleisstraat 135** ☎ **623 5142** 🚊 **1, 2, 4, 5, 6, 9, 13, 14, 16, 17, 24, 25**

Waterstone's

Branch of the British chain, with a huge stock of hardbacks and paperbacks, fiction and non-fiction, for adults and children.

✉ **Kalverstraat 152** ☎ **638 3821** 🚊 **1, 2, 5**

Gifts & Children's Items

Gifts

BLGK
Showcase for a group of local jewellery designers, each one with a different contemporary approach, but all making a variety of notable pieces at reasonable prices.

 Hartenstraat 28 🕾 624 8154 🚋 6, 13, 14, 17

Blue Gold Fish
Storehouse of fantastical gifts of all sorts, including jewellery, ornaments, home fixtures, fabrics and miscellaneous items that don't fall into any easily defined category.

✉ Rozengracht 17 🕾 623 3134 🚋 6, 13, 14, 17

Galleria d'Arte Rinascimento
Across the canal from the Anne Frankhuis, this slightly eccentric shop sells both the finest De Porcelyne Fles Delftware, and cheap 'n' cheerful imitations.

✉ Prinsengracht 170 🕾 622 7509 🚋 6, 13, 14, 17

Heinen
Hand-painted De Koninklijke Fles Delft Blue and Tichelaars Makkumware, made by a father-and-son team of craftsmen.

✉ Spiegelgracht 13 🕾 421 8360 🚋 1, 2, 5, 6, 13, 17

Het Kantenhuis
Most lace you can buy in Holland is machine-made, often even in other countries. This shop sells the genuine article – first-rate, superior, handmade Dutch lace.

✉ Kalverstraat 124 🕾 624 8618 🚋 4, 9, 14, 16, 24, 25

Parfumerie Douglas
Cut straight to the essence, amid a vast stock of big-name scents alongside other unpretentious concoctions and precocious wannabes.

✉ Beethovenstraat 30 🕾 679 0713 🚋 2, 3, 5, 12

La Savonnerie
Get into a lather over designer soap in arty and kitschy forms; it seems a downright shame actually to put some of it in a bath!

✉ Prinsengracht 294 🕾 428 1139 🚋 6, 13, 14, 17

Children's Wear & Toys

Kinderfeestwinkel
All kinds of fun things for kids to play with and wear at party time.

✉ Eerste van der Helststraat 13–15 🕾 672 2215 🚋 16, 24, 25

Mechanisch Speelgoed
Batteries definitely not included in these modern versions of toys from a kinder, gentler era of youthful playthings.

✉ Westerstraat 67 🕾 638 1680 🚋 3, 10

Oilily
Bright and sporty designer clothes for kids – an instant hit.

✉ P C Hooftstraat 131–3 🕾 672 3361 🚋 2, 3, 5, 12

Pas-Destoel
Brings interior design skills and a sense of fun to bear on children's furniture, room fittings and accessories.

✉ Westerstraat 260 🕾 420 7542 🚋 3, 10

Shoppers' Tips
• Most shops are open Mon 1–6 (department stores from 11), Tue–Wed and Fri 9–6, Thu 9–9, Sat 9–5; some are open Sun noon–5.

• For bargains, look out for *solden* (sales) during January and July; stickers on some goods saying *korting* (reduction); and on shop windows *totaal uitverkoop* (clearing out) when a shop is closing down or changing its lines.

• When you walk into a small shop to browse around, remember to greet the owner, a polite gesture Dutch people appreciate.

105

Department Stores, Malls & Markets

Dutch Gifts
Among items that make great souvenirs and gifts are: tulip bulbs (you may need a phyto-sanitary certificate to import them); bottles of *jenever* (Dutch gin); antiques; diamonds; cheese (not only Edam and Gouda); handmade pralines; crystal from Royal Leerdam; pewter; Delftware and Makkumware porcelain; clogs; prints; posters, and even postcards, from museum shops, depicting paintings and other exhibits.

Department Stores & Malls

De Bijenkorf
Flagship, up-market department store.
✉ **Dam 1** ☎ **552 1700** 🚊 **4, 9, 14, 16, 24, 25**

Hema
Cheap 'n' cheerful bargain basement chain. Good for underwear, household goods and some food items.
✉ **Kalvertoren Shopping Centre, Singel 457/A1** ☎ **422 8988** 🚊 **4, 9, 14, 16, 24, 25**

Magna Plaza
The turreted, Gothic, former main post office, known as 'Perenberg' (Pear Mountain), is now a fancy mall with shops and cafés on several floors.
✉ **Nieuwezijds Voorburgwal 182** ☎ **626 9199** 🚊 **1, 2, 5, 6, 13, 14, 17**

Maison de Bonneterie
Up-market store for clothing, shoes, household goods, sports equipment and more.
✉ **Kalverstraat 183/Rokin 140–2** ☎ **531 3400** 🚊 **4, 9, 14, 16, 24, 25**

Metz & Co
This *belle époque* building hosts a quality store with an avant-garde past, though its Rietveld furniture is now reproduction rather than original. Good for fabrics.
✉ **Keizersgracht 455/Leidsestraat 34–6** ☎ **520 7020** 🚊 **1, 2, 5**

Vroom & Dreesmann
Clothing, jewellery, perfumes, electronic and household goods.
✉ **Kalverstraat 203** ☎ **0900/235 8363** 🚊 **4, 9, 14, 16, 24, 25**

Markets

Albert Cuypmarkt
The city's biggest and most colourful street market: a long double-row of stalls selling foodstuffs, clothes, flowers, cakes and biscuits, household goods and more.
✉ **Albert Cuypstraat** 🕐 **Mon–Sat 10–5** 🚊 **4, 16, 24, 25**

Bloemenmarkt
Amsterdam's famous floating Flower Market, on a line of barges beside Muntplein (► 39).
✉ **Singel** 🕐 **Mon–Sat 9:30–5:30 (5 Sat)** 🚊 **4, 9, 14, 16, 24, 25**

Boerenmarkt
Saturday Farmer's Market selling organic produce, bread and cheese, and New Age jewellery, scents and health-care products.
✉ **Noordermarkt** 🕐 **Sat 9–4 (3 in winter)** 🚊 **1, 2, 5, 6, 13, 17**

Kunstmart Thorbeckeplein
Bijou paintings, pottery and sculpture at an elegant little Sunday art market.
✉ **Thorbeckeplein** 🕐 **Mar–Nov Sun 10:30–6** 🚊 **4, 9, 14**

Waterlooplein Fleemarkt
Once a standby of the city's Jewish community, this big flea market is sure to have something of interest.
✉ **Waterlooplein** 🕐 **Mon–Sat 9–5** 🚇 **Waterlooplein** 🚊 **9, 14**

Westermarkt
Similar to the Albert Cuypmarkt (► above), but on a more intimate scale.
✉ **Westerstraat** 🕐 **Mon–Sat 9–5** 🚊 **1, 2, 5, 6, 13, 17**

Food & Drink

J G Beune
Sells chocolate versions of Amsterdammertjes (the distinctive bollards that stop cars from parking on the pavement) and a colourful array of cakes and other goodies.

✉ **Haarlemmerdijk 156–8** ☎ **624 8356** 🚊 **1, 2, 5, 6, 13, 17**

De Bierkoning
You ought to find something to your taste among 950 different kinds of beer from all over the world, many of which come with their own accompanying glass.

✉ **Paleisstraat 125** ☎ **625 2336** 🚊 **1, 2, 5, 6, 13, 14, 17**

Eichholtz
Highly regarded delicatessen with Dutch, Amercian and other international specialities.

✉ **Leidsestraat 48** ☎ **622 0305** 🚊 **1, 2, 5**

Geels & Co
Heady aromas mark Holland's oldest tea and coffee traders, in a traditional setting with a tea and coffee museum attached.

✉ **Warmoesstraat 67** ☎ **624 0683** 🚊 **4, 9, 14, 16, 24, 25**

Hendrikse Patisserie
Purveyors of luscious cakes and pastries to the royal court – and fortunately to ordinary citizens, also.

✉ **Overtoom 472** ☎ **618 0472** 🚊 **1, 6**

Jacob Hooij
A medley of fragrant scents greets you as you enter this 1743 apothecary, selling herbs, spices, herbal teas, health foods, natural cosmetics and homeopathic medicines.

✉ **Kloveniersburgwal 12** ☎ **624 3041** Ⓜ **Nieuwmarkt**

Olivaria
Fine olive oils from around the world

✉ **Hazenstraat 2a** ☎ **638 3552** 🚊 **7, 10**

Patisserie Pompadour
A vast selection of delectable cakes and pastries, and an elegant tea room in which to consume those that you don't haul away.

✉ **Huidenstraat 12** ☎ **623 9554** 🚊 **1, 2, 5**

Vitals Vitamin Advice Shop
Vitamins, minerals and a range of food supplements.

✉ **Nieuwe Nieuwstraat 47** ☎ **625 7298** 🚊 **1, 2, 5, 6, 13, 17,**

H P De Vreng en Zoon
Decorated with 15,000 miniature bottles, this distillery and liquor store has been producing traditional *jenever* and liqueurs since 1852.

✉ **Nieuwendijk 75** ☎ **624 4581** 🚊 **1, 2, 5, 6, 13, 17**

De Waterwinkel
Cool reservoir of the world's bottled waters, from nifty designer H_2O to the aquatic equivalent of finest champagne.

✉ **Roelof Hartstraat 10** ☎ **675 5932** 🚊 **3, 12, 24**

Wout Arxhoek
One of the city's best cheese shops, with over 250 different varieties to choose from – imported from around the world as well as Dutch.

✉ **Damstraat 19** ☎ **622 9118** 🚊 **4, 9, 14, 16, 24, 25**

Diamonds' Best Friends
Buying diamonds can be a tricky business. Although they are far from being the only reputable diamond shops in Amsterdam, these five provide an 18-carat guarantee of quality:

Amsterdam Diamond Center
✉ Rokin 1–5
☎ 624 5787
🚊 4, 9, 14, 16, 24, 25

Coster Diamonds
✉ Paulus Potterstraat 2–6
☎ 305 5555
🚊 2, 5

Gassan Diamonds
✉ Nieuwe Uilenburgerstraat 173–5
☎ 622 5333
Ⓜ Waterlooplein
🚊 9, 14

Stoeltie Diamonds
✉ Wagenstraat 13–17
☎ 623 7601
Ⓜ Waterlooplein
🚊 4, 9, 14

Van Moppes Diamonds
✉ Albert Cuypstraat 2–6
☎ 676 1242
🚊 16, 24, 25

Fashion, Household & Speciality

Tax-free Shopping

If you live outside the European Union, you are entitled to a refund of 13.5 per cent of value-added tax (BTW) on purchases of €137 or more in one shop in a day. You can also make purchases above that amount in other shops, going through the refund process each time. You can identify participating shops by their 'tax-free shopping' stickers. Ask for an Easy Tax Free Cheque when you pay. When you are leaving Holland for a non-EU country, within three months of buying, present the cheque at Customs, who will stamp it. You can claim your refund at the International Cash Refund Office of Global Refund at Schiphol Airport, and by post to Global Refund Holland:

✉ Leidsevaartweg 99, 2106 AS Heemstede, Netherlands ☎ 023/524 1909.

Fashion & Accessories

Candy Corson

All kinds of quality leather accessories, with the emphasis on bags and belts.

✉ Sint-Luciënsteeg 19 ☎ 624 8061 🚊 1, 2, 5

Cora Kemperman

Elegant and imaginative, individually designed women's fashion.

✉ Leidsestraat 72 ☎ 625 1284 🚊 1, 2, 5

Emporio Armani

Exactly as you'd expect, quality and style in Italian clothing.

✉ P C Hooftstraat 39–41 ☎ 471 1121 🚊 2, 3, 5, 12

Hair Police

Hair styling in a variety of street-smart looks, along with more punky fashions, cosmetics and other accessories.

✉ Kerkstraat 113 ☎ 420 5841 🚊 1, 2, 5

Hester van Eeghen

Imaginatively designed leather accessories, including handbags, belts and wallets.

✉ Hartenstraat 1 ☎ 626 9212 🚊 6, 13, 14, 17

The Madhatter

Far-out headwear by local designers.

✉ Van der Helstplein 4 ☎ 664 7748 🚊 3, 12, 25

Oger

Quality men's clothing, including Ermenegildo Zegna.

✉ P C Hooftstraat 79–83 ☎ 676 8695 🚊 2, 3, 5, 12

Palette

Tiny shop with a big choice of well-made shoes in satin and silk.

✉ Nieuwezijds Voorburgwal 125 ☎ 639 3207 🚊 4, 9, 14, 16, 24, 25

Webers Holland

Sexy, humorous and avant-garde fashion, mainly for women.

✉ Kloveniersburgwal 26 ☎ 638 1777 🚇 Nieuwmarkt 🚊 4, 9, 14, 16, 24, 25

Alternative

Absolute Danny

Erotic clothing and accessories with a sense of style.

✉ Oudezijds Achterburgwal 78 ☎ 421 0915 🚊 4, 9, 14, 16, 24, 25

Condomerie Het Gulden Vlies

The world's first specialist condom shop, the 'Golden Fleece' stocks an impressive range of this singular item of apparel.

✉ Warmoesstraat 141 ☎ 627 4174 🚊 4, 9, 14, 16, 24, 25

The Headshop

Market leader since the heady summer of 1968 in drug paraphernalia and books, oriental clothing, weird and wonderful jewellery, insight into magic mushrooms and more along the same lines.

✉ Kloveniersburgwal 39 ☎ 624 9061 🚇 Nieuwmarkt

Hemp Works

Clothing, cosmetics and more, all made from multipurpose hemp fibre.

✉ Nieuwendijk 13 ☎ 421 1762 🚊 1, 2, 5, 6, 13, 17

Household

Kitsch Kitchen
If you want your kitchen filled with all kinds of brightly coloured, odd-looking stuff from around the world, this is the place to get it.
✉ **Eerste Bloemdwarsstraat 21** ☎ **428 4969** 🚊 **6, 13, 14, 17**

Outras Coisas
Furnishings and acessories in traditional styles for the home and garden, both new and secondhand, originate from around the world.
✉ **Herenstraat 31** ☎ **625 7281** 🚊 **1, 2, 5, 6, 13, 17**

Wonen 2000
You likely won't be able to haul away many of the larger items from this vast depository of designer furniture, but the range of portable accessories is extensive too.
✉ **Rozengracht 219–223** ☎ **521 8710** 🚊 **6, 13, 14, 17**

World of Wonders
Interior design store in the fast-gentrifying Eastern Docks, with up-market fabrics and furnishings, and many small items to enliven your living space.
✉ **KNSM-laan 293–9** ☎ **418 4067** 🚌 **Bus 32**

Speciality

Animation Art
Drawings, paintings and figurines of famous cartoon characters from Superman to Tintin and the Smurfs.
✉ **Berenstraat 39** ☎ **627 7600** 🚊 **1, 2, 5**

Bankras
One of the best bicycle shops in this bike-mad city.
✉ **Nieuwe Hoogstraat 21–3** ☎ **624 6137** 🚇 **Nieuwmarkt**

Capsicum
Fabrics to go – anywhere and with anything. Choose from delicate material for summer dresses to hard-wearing furniture covers.
✉ **Oude Hoogstraat 1** ☎ **623 1016** 🚊 **4, 9, 14, 16, 24, 25**

Cortina Paper
The paper chase ends here, in a stockpile of all kinds of fine paper, including handmade, as well as notebooks and other writing and sketching materials.
✉ **Reestraat 22** ☎ **623 6676** 🚊 **6, 13, 14, 17**

P G C Hajenius
Treats smoking reverently rather than as a social nuisance, with a big range of pipes and cigars.
✉ **Rokin 92–6** ☎ **623 7494** 🚊 **4, 9, 14, 16, 24, 25**

Hera Kaarsen
Candles that it seems a pity to burn, many of them being works of waxen art designed by the owners.
✉ **Overtoom 402** ☎ **616 2886** 🚊 **1, 6**

Ivy
For a special and elegant bouquet of flowers that's more (much more) than the traditional bunch of 10 tulips.
✉ **Leidseplein 35** ☎ **623 6561** 🚊 **1, 2, 5, 6, 7, 10**

Otten & Zn
Some Dutch people still clomp around in wooden *klompen* (clogs). This shop sells fine wearable ones as well as souvenirs.
✉ **Eerste van der Helstraat 31** ☎ **662 9724** 🚊 **16, 24, 25**

Fast Getaways
If you don't want to spend your valuable time in the city shopping, and if you're leaving from Schiphol Airport, do it there. With 40 shops stocking 120,000 different items in the airport's duty-free section, and another 40 non-duty-free shops at Schiphol Plaza, there's no shortage of choice.

109

Attractions for Children

Getting around

Trams are a must, in particular older trams in which kids can stand beside the driver. Canal boat cruises and free passenger ferries behind Centraal Station can also be fun.

Should you let children cycle? There are bicycle lanes, but there are also trams, heavy traffic, lots of other cyclists, and unthinking pedestrians. It may be safer to take them on an out-of-town cycling trip, such as the one to Ouderkerk aan de Amstel (➤ 85).

Museums

The Rijksmuseum's Golden Age masterpieces (➤ 22–3) may glaze youthful eyes. Child-friendly exhibits, such as the beautifully made doll's houses, should go down better.

Older children will appreciate the special atmosphere at the Anne Frankhuis, the teenage Jewish diarist's wartime hideaway (➤ 17). Younger ones are liable to be bored, as there is not much to see.

Sail in to the fabled Spice Islands aboard a replica 17th-century Dutch East Indiaman at the Nederlands Scheepvaartmuseum (➤ 60), and in summer watch actors re-create scenes of onboard . Interactive science and technology museum NEMO (➤ 61), and Kindermuseum TM Junior (☎ 568 8300), the children-only section of the Tropenmuseum (➤ 73), should fascinate switched-on children.

Children's Farms and Zoos

Artis (➤ 35), as well as being a great zoo, has a children's farm with goats, a cow, a donkey and chickens, where children get an insight into life on a real farm. The same experience applies to a children's farm in the Pijp district, Kinderboerderij De Pijp (✉ Lizzy Ansinghstraat 82 ☎ 664 8303 ⊙ Mon–Fri 11–5, Sat–Sun 1–5 🚊 12, 25). More of an urban petting zoo is the tiny Stadsboerderij De Dierencapel (✉ Bickersgracht 207 ☎ 420 6855 ⊙ Tue–Sun 9–4:30 🚌 Bus 18, 22) in the Western Islands.

Play Time

What to do when it rains? You can take children aged 1–12 to TunFun, a big, multi-attraction indoor play park near Waterlooplein, with one adult accompanying up to four children (✉ Mr Visserplein 7 ☎ 689 4300 ⊙ Daily 10–7 🚊 Waterlooplein 🚊 9, 14

Places of Interest

In addition to such Dutch favourites as soccer hotshot Johann Cruyff, there's a gallery of waxwork international names at Madame Tussaud's (➤ 56). You can get the lowdown on Cruyff's glorious career and that of his former team, Ajax, at the Ajax Museum at the superb Amsterdam ArenA Stadium in Amsterdam-Zuidoost (✉ ArenA Boulevard 3 ☎ 311 1333 ⊙ Daily 1-hour guided tour 10–5 🚊 Bijlmer/ArenA). Many city-centre bell towers have carillons that break into tinkling song at intervals. You can hear carillon concerts at the Westertoren (➤ 26 – ⊙ Tue noon–1); Zuidertoren (➤ 75 – ⊙ Thu noon–1); Munttoren (➤ 57 – ⊙ Fri noon–1); Oude Kerkstoren (➤ 63 – ⊙ Sat 4–5). Open-Air Chess (✉ Max Euweplein), off Leidseplein, played with big plastic pieces, should appeal to cerebral exhibitionists. For shoot-'em-up action, try Intersphere Lasergames (✉ Prins Hendrikkade 194 ☎ 622 4809 🚊 22, 32). White-knuckle go-kart racing thrills are on offer at Kartbaan Amsterdam (✉ Theemsweg 19, Sloterdijk ☎ 611 1642 🚊 12).

Beach and Sea

Zandvoort (► 89) is Amsterdam's closest and busiest resort and has a great beach, safe bathing and lots to do. Resorts north of Zandvoort are quieter, with fewer amenities.

The freshwater IJsselmeer lake (► 84) used to be a sea. It's not ideal for swimming, although paddling in shallow water should be alright, but there are old harbours, traditional sailing ships and boat excursions.

Windmills

Amsterdam is not well-endowed with these emblematic Dutch sights. You'd do better at nearby De Zaanse Schans (► 88), and even better to make the longer trip to Kinderdijk (► 87), near Rotterdam.

Flowers

Taking the kids to the Bulb Fields (► 78), Keukenhof Garden (► 78), and the Floating Flower Market (► 106) will probably turn out to be one of those gender things. Boys will probably love them and girls hate them – you never know, it could happen.

Sports

For swimming, ice-skating, fishing, and more (► 115).

Theme Parks

Archeon

Step into the past at this archaeological theme park between Amsterdam and Rotterdam, which re-creates scenes from Stone Age, ancient Roman and medieval life, and tells the story of the Earth from its formation.

🖂 **Archeonlaan 1, Alphen aan**

den Rijn ☎ 0172/447 744 🕓 May–Oct Tue–Sun 10–5; Jul–Aug daily 10–6 🚉 Alphen aan de Rijn ♿ Good 🍽 Very expensive

Dolfinarium Harderwijk

Europe's largest dolphinarium puts on fabulous shows, runs research programmes and has a rehabilitation centre for sick and injured creatures. In addition to open-air pools there are glass tanks where you can view the performers underwater.

🖂 **Strandboulevard Oost 1, Harderwijk** ☎ 0341/467 400 🕓 Mid-Feb–Oct daily 10–6 🚉 Harderwijk ♿ Good 🍽 Very expensive

De Efteling

Rather further afield, near Den Bosch in southern Holland, De Efteling is one of Europe's oldest theme parks with rides and roller-coasters and the fairytale forest for younger children.

🖂 **Europalaan 1, Kaatsheuvel** ☎ 0416/288 111 🕓 Apr–Oct, daily 10–6 (mid–Jul to end Aug till midnight) 🍽 Expensive

Circus

If you don't think your children can perform enough tricks already, let them learn tightrope walking, juggling and other circus tricks at Circus Elleboog.

🖂 **Passeerdersgracht 32** ☎ 626 9370 🕓 Mon–Fri 10–5, Sat 1:30–5, Sun 10:30–4 🚊 7, 10,

Theatre

There are mime and puppet shows at nearby De Krakeling Theater.

🖂 **Nieuwe Passeerdersstraat 1** ☎ 625 3824 🕓 Mon–Fri 11–4, Sat–Sun 2–7 🚊 7, 10

Eating Out

There are McDonalds, Burger King, KFC and Pizza Hut outlets all over town. For a different kind of taste sensation, where children aged five to 12 cook for themselves supervised by adults, take them to Kinderkookkafé (🖂 Oudezijds Achterburgwal 193 ☎ 625 3257 🕓 Sat cooking 3:30–6, dinner 6–8 (age 8 plus); Sun cooking 2:30–5, high tea 5–6 (age 5 plus); Mon–Fri 1–3 🚇 Nieuwmarkt 🚊 4, 9, 14, 16, 24, 25).

Music, Theatre, Dance & Cinema

Information and Tickets

For information on, and tickets for, events at most city venues, visit Amsterdams Uit Buro (AUB) ✉ Leidseplein 26 🕐 Daily 10–6 (Thu until 9) 🚊 1, 2, 5, 6, 7, 10, 20; or call the AUB-Uitlijn ☎ 0900/0191 🕐 Daily 9–9. You can also buy tickets at VVV tourist offices.

For programme information, the VVV's monthly English-language guide, *Amsterdam Day by Day*, provides extensive listings across the range of cultural events, as does the free monthly Dutch *Uitkrant*, which you find at many venues.

Beurs van Berlage

Home of the Netherlands Philharmonic Orchestra and Netherlands Chamber Orchestra, in the former stock exchange.
✉ Damrak 243 ☎ 521 7500 🕐 Box office: Tue–Fri 12:30–6, Sat 12:30–5, and 1¼ hours before performances 🚊 4, 9, 14, 16, 24, 25

Concertgebouw

Home of the famed Royal Concertgebouw Orchestra. Its Grote Zaal is considered one of the world's most acoustically perfect concert halls; the Kleine Zaal is used mainly for chamber music and recitals. Free concerts Wednesdays at 12:30.
✉ Concertgebouwplein 2–6 ☎ 671 8345 🕐 Box office: daily 10–5 for advance purchase 🚊 3, 5, 12, 16

De IJsbreker

The place for contemporary, electronic, experimental, cutting-edge music. It is due to move to new Muziek-gebouw (► below) in 2005.
✉ Weesperzijde 23 ☎ 693 9093 🕐 Box office: Mon–Fri 10–5 🚇 Weesperplein 🚊 3, 6, 7, 10

Muziekgebouw

Due to open in 2005, this new concert hall on the IJ waterfront will house the De IJsbreker modern music centre, the Bimhuis jazz club and other musical ventures.
✉ Amstel 1–3 ☎ 625 5455 🕐 Box office: Mon–Sat 10–6, Sun 11:30–6 🚇 Waterlooplein 🚊 9, 14

Muziektheater

Home of the Netherlands Opera and National Ballet, and Amsterdam venue for performances by The Hague's highly regarded Netherlands Dance Theatre.
✉ Amstel 1–3 ☎ 625 5455 🕐 Box office: Mon–Sat 10–6, Sun 11:30–6 🚇 Waterlooplein 🚊 9, 14

Recitals

Engelse Kerk
✉ Begijnhof 48 ☎ 624 9665 🚊 1, 2, 5

Nieuwe Kerk
✉ Dam ☎ 638 6909 🚊 1, 2, 4, 5,6, 9, 13, 14, 16, 17, 24, 25

Oude Kerk
✉ Oudekerksplein ☎ 625 8284 🚊 4, 9, 14, 16, 24, 25

Waalse Kerk
✉ Oudezijds Achterburgwal 157 ☎ 623 2074 🚊 4, 9, 14, 16, 24, 25

Theatre, Dance & Musicals

Koninklijke Theater Carré
Dutch versions of big-name musicals, cabaret, pop music.
✉ Amstel 115–25 ☎ 0800/2525 255 🕐 Box office: Mon–Sat 10–7, Sun 1–7 🚇 Weesperplein 🚊 4, 6, 7, 10

Stadsschouwburg
Mainstream Dutch theatre, and an occasional touring performance in English. Also hosts opera and dance.
✉ Leidseplein 26 ☎ 624 2311 🕐 Mon–Sat 10am–6; Sun & pub hols from 90 mins before performance 🚊 1, 2, 5, 6, 7, 10

Vondelpark Openluchttheater
Open-air theatre, music and dance in summer.
✉ Vondelpark ☎ 523 7700 🚊 1, 2, 3, 5, 6, 12 🎫 Free

Live Music

Alto Jazz Café
Wide-ranging music from resident and visiting combos.
✉ **Korte Leidsedwarsstraat 115** ☎ 626 3249 🚊 1, 2, 5, 6, 7, 10

Bimhuis
The place for serious lovers of improvisational jazz. Due to move to the Muziekgebouw in 2005.
✉ **Oudeschans 73–7** ☎ 623 1361 🚇 **Waterlooplein** 🚊 9, 14

De Heeren van Aemstel
Upper-crust café where you occasionally catch some big names at their session on Wednesday at 9:30.
✉ **Thorbeckeplein 5** ☎ 620 2173 🚊 4, 9, 14,

Dance Clubs & Discos

Akhnaton
World music, salsa, rap and reggae.
✉ **Nieuwezijds Kolk 25** ☎ 624 3396 🚊 1, 2, 5, 6, 13, 17

To Dance
In the atmospheric and extensive setting of a former orphanage chapel (▶ 100), dance to a mix of funk, soul and galactic disco. Friday and Saturday are the nostalgia evenings, with music dating from as far back as the '60s.
✉ **Club Arena, 's Grave-sandestraat 51** ☎ 633 3021 🚊 3, 7, 10

iT
Dance club, with techno and house in a wild-party mood. Saturday is gay night.
✉ **Amstelstraat 24** ☎ 625 0111 🚊 4, 9, 14,

Odeon
Dance club in a 17th-century canalhouse.
✉ **Singel 460** ☎ 624 9711 🚊 1, 2, 5

Paradiso
Rock, reggae and pop, live and disco, in a former church.
✉ **Weteringschans 6–8** ☎ 626 4521 🚊 1, 2, 5, 6, 7, 10

House of Soul
Late-night house, garage, utopia and soul.
✉ **Amstelstraat 28–32** ☎ 620 2333 🚊 4, 9, 14

Rock Music
Big names perform at Ajax soccer club's Amsterdam ArenA stadium (▶ 115); less-big acts at Koninklijke Theater Carré (▶ 112).

Cinemas
Most films are in the original language with Dutch subtitles.

City
Seven screens just off Leidseplein.
✉ **Kleine Gartmanplantsoen 13–25** ☎ 623 4579 🚊 1, 2, 5, 6, 7, 10

Nederlands Filmmuseum Cinematheek
International, art-house and rarely screened films.
✉ **Vondelpark 3** ☎ 589 1400 🚊 1, 2, 3, 5, 6, 12,

Pathé ArenA
Eight screens next to Ajax football stadium.
✉ **ArenA Boulevard 600** ☎ 0900 1458 🚇 **Bijlmer/ArenA**

Tuschinski Theater
Superb, art deco cinema complex with six screens.
✉ **Reguliersbreestraat 26–8** ☎ 626 2633 🚊 4, 9, 14

The Milky Way
It's not easy to define De Melkweg, a multipurpose, multimedia, multicultural club in an old dairy factory – hence the name. It started life as a hippie hangout during the 1960s and has kept up with most cultural trends in the city ever since. Alphabetically speaking, it's an art centre, café, dance hall, discothèque, exhibition space, library, restaurant and theatre. Philosophically speaking, it's a temple of alternative culture. You need to take out a cheap, temporary membership to get in.
✉ **Lijnbaansgracht 234a** ☎ 531 8181 🚊 1, 2, 5, 6, 7, 10

Brown Cafés & Proeflokalen

Gay Amsterdam
The city takes some pride in its status as Europe's gay capital, and there are many clubs, cafés and resources for gay and lesbian residents and visitors. For information, contact the gay people's organisation COC (✉ Rozenstraat 14 ☎ 623 4079 🚋 6, 13, 14, 17, or the Gay and Lesbian Switchboard ☎ 623 6565).

Brown Cafés
A *bruine kroeg* (brown café) is an old-style Amsterdam bar, with walls smoked brown over the centuries, an unhurried approach to life, and almost a guarantee of friendly conversation.

De Druif
Nautically oriented waterfront bar from 1631 in the Eastern Dock area.
✉ **Rapenburgerplein 83**
☎ **624 4530** 🚌 **Bus 22**

De Engelbewaarder
Jazz on Sunday from 4PM livens up a usually tranquil, arty hang-out.
✉ **Kloveniersburgwal 59**
☎ **625 3772** Ⓜ **Nieuwmarkt**
🚋 **4, 9, 14, 16, 24, 25**

Hoppe
Standing room only when young professionals and barfly academics drop in for a quick one, or two, after work. The building dates from 1670.
✉ **Spuistraat 18–20** ☎ **420 4420** 🚋 **1, 2, 5**

De Karpershoek
Doesn't seem to have changed much since opening in 1629, when its customers were herring packers, sailors and dockers.
✉ **Martelaarsgracht 2** ☎ **624 7886** 🚋 **1, 2, 5, 6, 13, 17**

't Loosje
Turn-of-the-19th-century bar that used to be a horse-drawn tram waiting room.
✉ **Nieuwmarkt 32–4** ☎ **627 2635** Ⓜ **Nieuwmarkt**

Papeneiland
Traditional Amsterdam café, seemingly unchanged since 1642.

✉ **Prinsengracht 2** ☎ **624 1989** 🚋 **1, 2, 5, 6, 13, 17**

De Reiger
Artists, students and others of that ilk are the main customers of this restful Jordaan watering-hole.
✉ **Nieuwe Leliestraat 34**
☎ **624 7426** 🚋 **10, 13, 14, 17**

Reijnders
Traditional café on Leidse-plein, a square where antique charm has mostly given way to modern frenzy.
✉ **Leidseplein 6** ☎ **623 4419**
🚋 **1, 2, 5, 6, 7, 10**

't Smalle
Originally a *proeflokaal* (▶ below), this cosy café has a terrace on the canal.
✉ **Egelantiersgracht 12**
☎ **623 9617** 🚋 **13, 14, 17**

Tabac
Tiny, wood-floored café on the corner of Prinsengracht.
✉ **Brouwersgracht 101**
☎ **622 4413** 🚌 **Bus 18, 22**

Proeflokalen
'Tasting houses' were established by *jenever* distillers to allow customers a free sample before buying. Today, sadly, you have to pay.

De Drie Fleschjes
Rows of padlocked wooden kegs line a wall in the 'Three Little Bottles', from 1650.
✉ **Gravenstraat 18** ☎ **624 8443** 🚋 **1, 2, 4, 5, 9, 13, 14, 16, 24, 25**

De Ooievaar
Holland's smallest tasting house produces and sells its own-brand *jenevers*.
✉ **Sint Olofspoort 1** ☎ **420 8004** 🚋 **1, 2, 4, 5, 9, 13, 16, 17, 24, 25**

Sport

American Football

Amsterdam Admirals
The Admirals, home-based at Ajax's soccer stadium, play this popular sport in the Dutch league.
✉ ArenA Boulevard ☎ 311 1333 🚇 Bijlmer/ArenA

Cricket

Amsterdamse Cricket Club & VRA
Watch the city's two cricket teams in action on alternate summer Sundays.
✉ Nieuwe Kalfjeslaan 21b, Amsterdamse Bos ☎ 643 4438 🚌 Bus 170, 171, 172

Fitness
These two fitness centres have gym, sauna, solarium and aerobics classes.

Fitness Aerobic Center Jansen
✉ Rokin 109–11 ☎ 626 9366 🕐 Mon–Fri 10AM–10:30PM, Sat–Sun 12–8 🚊 4, 9, 14, 16, 24, 25

A Bigger Splash
✉ Looiersgracht 26–30 ☎ 624 8484 🕐 7AM to midnight 🚊 7, 10

Football

Ajax
Amsterdam's crack soccer squad play at a superb new stadium in Amsterdam Zuidoost.
✉ Amsterdam ArenA, ArenA Boulevard ☎ 311 1333 🚇 Bijlmer/ArenA

Golf

Golfbaan Waterland
An 18-hole course in Amsterdam-Noord.
✉ Buikslotermeerdijk 141 ☎ 636 1010 🚌 Bus 30

Horse-riding

Amsterdamse Manege
Out-of-town riding school.
✉ Nieuwe Kalfjeslaan 25, Amsterdamse Bos ☎ 643 1342 🚌 Bus 170, 171, 172

Hollandsche Manege
Opened in 1882 and inspired by Vienna's Spanish Riding School.
✉ Vondelstraat 140 ☎ 618 0942 🚊 1, 6

Ice-skating
Canals often freeze in winter, turning waterways into a skating rink.

Jaap Eden Baan
Big outdoor circuit, with a side area for beginners.
✉ Radioweg 64 ☎ 694 9894 🚊 9

Swimming

Marnixbad
Regular-shaped, public pool.
✉ Marnixplein 9 ☎ 625 4843 🚊 3, 10

De Mirandabad
Clear-roofed building with wave machines, slides and other amenities.
✉ De Mirandalaan 9 ☎ 642 8080 🚊 25

Tennis

Amstelpark Tenniscentrum
Plenty of choice, with 42 outdoor and 10 indoor courts. All the outdoor ones are floodlit and available for night play.
✉ Koenenkade 8, Amsterdamse Bos ☎ 301 0700 🚌 Bus 170, 171, 172

Big Freeze
In years when the canals freeze, you may not have to 'restrict' yourself to skating through the city on these sparkling highways. Many Amsterdammers tour through the countryside and even skate on the IJsselmeer when the ice is solid enough. If you are tempted to join them, a good rule is never to go where Dutch people fear to skate – they have a lot of experience and know, usually, when conditions are safe.

What's On When

Amsterdam Arts Adventure

Amsterdam's main cultural season runs from September until June, which used to mean that the city was a cultural desert at the busiest time of the year for tourism. Arts Adventure fills the gap with a varied programme of mostly informal, often open-air, music, theatre and dance events from June to August. For information, contact VVV tourist offices and Amsterdam Uit Buro (➤ 112).

North Sea Jazz Festival

If you need an excuse to visit The Hague, this annual three-day shindig at the city's Nederlands Congres Centrum during July could be it. You'll hear many – if not most – of the big international names in jazz and blues, with more than a hundred concerts. For more information, contact the organisers: ☎ 015/215 7756; www.northseajazz.nl.

February

Pre-Lenten Carnival (early February): Amsterdam's has had a less than chequered career, because carnival-goers prefer Maastricht's.

March

Stille Omgang (Sunday nearest March 15): Catholic procession celebrating the 1345 'Miracle of the Host'. Keukenhof Garden (late March–late May): Beautiful gardens at Lisse open (➤ 78), as tulips and other spring flowers blossom.

April

National Museum Weekend (mid-month): Museums offer a free or reduced-price. *World Press Photo Awards* (Monday, mid-April): Amsterdam-based annual photojournalism prizes. *Koninginnedag* (April 30): Queen Beatrix's official birthday – massive street parties and free markets.

May

Herdenkingsdag (May 4): Remembrance Day for World War II victims; two-minute silence at 8PM. *Bevrijdingsdag* (May 5): Liberation Day celebrations; a less frenetic version of Koninginnedag. *National Windmill Day* (second Saturday): Windmills open to the public. *Vlaggetjesdag* (last Saturday): Flag Day fishing-boat race at Scheveningen (➤ 81) to bring back the season's first new herring for the Queen.

June

Amsterdam Roots Festival (early to mid-June): Festival of world music, dance, films, exhibits and workshops, at the Melkweg multimedia cultural central and others. *Canalhouse Gardens in Bloom* (mid-June): Private canalhouse gardens on Herengracht, Keizersgracht and Prinsen-gracht open to the public. *Holland Festival* (throughout June): International arts festival in Amsterdam, The Hague, Rotterdam and Utrecht.

July

Amsterdam Arts Adventure: ➤ panel. *North Sea Jazz Festival*: ➤ panel.

August

Prinsengracht Concert (penultimate Saturday): Pulitzer Hotel hosts classical music concert on a canal barge. *Uitmarkt* (last weekend): Cultural venues preview the new season.

September

Bloemencorso (first Saturday): Flower parade from Aalsmeer to Amsterdam. *Open Monumentendag* (second Saturday): Monuments and buildings that are usually closed or only partly open, are open.

November

Sinterklaas (third Saturday): Holland's Santa Claus parades through town.

December

Pakjesavond (December 5): Holland's traditional day for giving presents. *Oudejaarsavond* (December 31): Partying in the street and fireworks.

Practical Matters

Above: *bikes to go at a rental shop*
Right: *Canal Bus route map*

GMT	Amsterdam	Germany	USA (NY)	Spain
→	→	→	←	→
12 noon	1PM	1PM	7AM	1PM

BEFORE YOU GO

WHAT YOU NEED

● Required
○ Suggested
▲ Not required

Some countries require a passport to remain valid for a minimum period (usually at least six months) beyond the date of entry – contact their consulate or embassy or your travel agent for details.

	UK	Germany	USA	Spain
Passport or National Identity Card where applicable	●	●	●	●
Visa (Regulations can change – check before your journey)	▲	▲	▲	▲
Onward or Return Ticket	▲	▲	▲	▲
Health Inoculations	▲	▲	▲	▲
Health Documentation (reciprocal agreement document, ➤ 123, Health)	●	●	●	●
Travel Insurance	○	○	○	○
Driving Licence (national)	●	●	●	●
Car Insurance Certificate (if own car)	○	○	○	○
Car Registration Document (if own car)	●	●	●	●

WHEN TO GO

Amsterdam

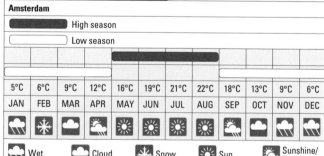

High season

Low season

5°C	6°C	9°C	12°C	16°C	19°C	21°C	22°C	18°C	13°C	9°C	6°C
JAN	FEB	MAR	APR	MAY	JUN	JUL	AUG	SEP	OCT	NOV	DEC

 Wet   Cloud   Snow   Sun   Sunshine/Showers

TOURIST OFFICES

In the UK
Netherlands Board of
Tourism (NBT)
PO Box 30783
London WC2B 6DH
☎ 020 7539 7953
fax: 020 7539 7953
wwwgo.holland.com/uk

In the USA
Netherlands Board of
Tourism (NBT)
355 Lexington Avenue
New York
NY 10017
☎ 212/557 3500
fax: 212/370 9507
www.goholland.com/us

POLICE 112

FIRE 112

ANY EMERGENCY (including AMBULANCE) 112

ROAD ASSISTANCE (ANWB Wegenwacht) 0800 0888

WHEN YOU ARE THERE

ARRIVING

There are direct flights from Europe and North America. Dutch airline KLM (☎ 474 7747) has scheduled flights from Britain, mainland Europe, North America and beyond, to Amsterdam Airport Schiphol. There are ferry services between Britain and IJmuiden, Rotterdam Europoort and Hoek van Holland. High-speed trains connect Amsterdam with Paris, Brussels and Cologne, and there are international trains and buses from many European cities.

Amsterdam Airport Schiphol	Journey times
Distance to city centre	
12 kilometres	14–19 minutes
	20 minutes
	30 minutes

MONEY

The currency of the Netherlands is the euro. There are banknotes for 5, 10, 20, 50, 100, 200 and 500 euros, and coins for 1, 2, 5, 10, 20 and 50 cents, and 1 and 2 euros.

Change money at banks and bureaux de change. Grenswisselkantoor (GWK), with exchange offices at Schiphol airort, Centraal Station and many other main railway stations, ports and motorway border crossings offer fair deals but other bureaux de change may not. Although traveller's cheques are accepted at some hotels, restaurants and shops, it is more advantageous to change them at banks or GWK offices.

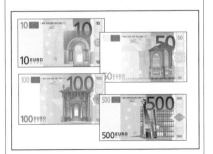

TIME

 Holland is on Central European Time (GMT+1). Dutch Summer Time (GMT+2) operates from late March, when clocks are put forward one hour, until late October.

CUSTOMS

 CUSTOMS ALLOWANCES

Goods Bought Outside the EU (Duty-Free Limits):
Alcohol: 1 litre of spirits over 22% volume, OR 2 litres of fortified wine, sparkling wine or other liqueurs, PLUS 2 litres of still table wine
Tobacco: 200 cigarettes, OR 100 cigarillos, OR 50 cigars, OR 250g of tobacco
Perfume: 50ml
Toilet water: 250ml

Goods Bought Inside the EU for Your Own Use (Guidance Levels):
Alcohol: 10 litres of spirits, AND 20 litres of fortified wine, sparkling wine or other liqueurs, AND 90 litres of wine, AND 110 litres of beer
Tobacco: 800 cigarettes, AND 400 cigarillos, AND 200 cigars, AND 1kg of tobacco

(For tobacco and alcohol allowances visitors must be 17 and over)

 NO Drugs, firearms, ammunition, offensive weapons, obscene material, unlicensed animals.

UK
Consulate ☎ 676 4343
Embassy ☎ 070/364 5800

Germany
Embassy ☎ 070/342 0600

USA
Consulate ☎ 664 5661
Embassy ☎ 070/310 9209

Spain
☎ 070/364 3166

WHEN YOU ARE THERE

TOURIST OFFICES

Holland Tourist Information (HTi)
Schiphol Plaza
Amsterdam Airport Schiphol
☎ 0900/400 4040
🕙 Daily 7AM–10PM

VVV (Vereniging voor Vreemdelingen Verkeer) is the universal name for Holland's tourist information organisations, with offices in every city and town.

VVV Amsterdam
✉ Postbus 3901
1001 AS Amsterdam
☎ 0900/400 4040
Fax: 625 2869
www.visitamsterdam.nl

Centraal Station
Platform 2 & Stationsplein 10
🕙 Daily 9–5 (later during summer and other peak periods)

Leidseplein 1
🕙 Daily 9–5 (later during summer and other peak periods)

NATIONAL HOLIDAYS

J	F	M	A	M	J	J	A	S	O	N	D
1		(3)	1(4)	1(3)	2						2

1 Jan	New Year's Day
Mar/Apr	Good Friday, Easter Sunday, Easter Monday
Apr/May	Ascension Day
30 Apr	Queen's Day
5 May	Liberation Day
May/Jun	Pentecost Sunday and Pentecost Monday
25 Dec	Christmas Day
26 Dec	Second Day of Christmas

Banks, businesses, most shops and some museums close on these days.

OPENING HOURS

○ Shops ● Museums/monuments
● Offices ○ Churches
● Banks ◐ Pharmacies

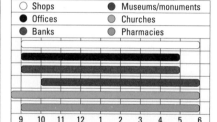

| 9 AM | 10 AM | 11 AM | 12 PM | 1 PM | 2 PM | 3 PM | 4 PM | 5 PM | 6 PM |

In addition to the times shown above, some shops close between noon and 2PM and all day Sunday and Monday, some do not open until 2PM on Monday, many stay open until 9PM on Thursday and close at 5PM on Saturday. Department stores and many other city-centre shops open from noon until 5PM on Sunday. Most supermarkets are open Monday to Friday from 8AM until 8PM, and 6PM on Saturday. Some food shops, often selling delicatessen food and cooked meals to take away in addition to foodstuffs, open from 5PM until midnight. Some banks close at 4PM rather than 5PM, some stay open until 7PM on Thursday, and some open on Saturday. Government offices open Monday to Friday from 8:30PM until 4PM.

DRIVE ON THE RIGHT

TOILETS CHARGE

★★ ★★

PUBLIC TRANSPORT

 Internal Flights Distances between Dutch cities are so short that air travel is rarely worth while, but KLM subsidiaries KLM Cityhopper and KLM Exel connect Amsterdam, Eindhoven, Enschede, Groningen and Maastricht.

 Trains Trains are the best way to get to many nearby destinations and for travel throughout the country. Nederlandse Spoorwegen trains are clean and punctual and its Intercity (IC) trains are fast (but not high speed).

 Trams It's hard to imagine Amsterdam without trams. The city's transport company, the Gemeentevervoerbedrijf (GVB), runs 17 tram lines; For public transport information, call (☎ 0900 9292).

Buses GVB buses complement the tram network and cover many points that trams don't serve. Connexxion buses handle regional services; they are generally slower than trains to common destinations, but serve many places that trains don't.

 Metro There are four Metro lines: 50, 51, 53 and 54. These lines serve the suburbs and are generally not useful for points within the city centre, except for Nieuwmarkt, which has no tram or bus service, and Waterlooplein.

 Boat Most canal boats are touring rather than transport options. For that you need Canal Bus (☎ 623 9886), Museum Boat (☎ 530 1090), which connects many popular museums and other attractions, and Water Taxi (☎ 530 1090).

CAR RENTAL

 The leading international companies have offices at Schiphol Airport and in town. Driving in Amsterdam is not recommended, as the city's narrow streets are congested, parking charges are high to discourage cars, and the penalties are high.

TAXIS

 Generally you cannot hail taxis on the street, although some will stop if you do. You can pick up taxis at the airport, main railway stations, busy city locations and outside bigger hotels. To call a cab, ring Taxi Centrale (☎ 677 7777).

DRIVING

 Speed limits on motorways (snelwegen) are 100km/h on ring roads, approaches to towns, and other busy stretches; 120km/h on other sections.

 Speed limits on country roads are 80km/h.

 Speed limits on urban roads are 50km/h.

 Seatbelts must be worn in front seats at all times and in rear seats where fitted.

 Random breath-testing. Never drive under the influence of alcohol.

 Petrol (benzine), is sold as Super: 98-octane leaded (lood); Super plus: 98-octane unleaded (loodvrij); and Euro: 95-octane unleaded. Diesel and liquid petroleum gas (autogas) are also available.

 If your car breaks down, contact ANWB Wegenwacht (+ 0800/0888). On motorways use the yellow-coloured emergency phones (every 2km) to contact the emergency breakdown service.

PERSONAL SAFETY

Opportunistic theft, such as pickpocketing and stealing from distracted or careless people, is prevalent and tourists are a prime target. Robbery with violence is much rarer, but still take sensible precautions:

- Avoid quiet places at night, particularly if you are alone.
- Watch out for your removables on trams, at Centraal Station, Schiphol Airport, in popular museums, at markets, and on the beach.
- Leave nothing visible in your car to tempt a thief.

Police (*politie*) assistance:
☎ **112**
from any call box

ELECTRICITY

The power supply in Amsterdam is 220 volts Sockets accept two-round-pin plugs. An

adaptor is needed for most non-Continental
appliances and a voltage transformer for appliances operating on 100–120 volts; exceptions are shavers that use 110-volt sockets you find in many hotel rooms.

TELEPHONES

Most public telephones accept KPN Telecom phonecards (telefoonkaarten) of €5, €13 and €25; some accept coins of 5, 10, 20 and 30 cents and €1 and €2; some accept both phonecards and coins;

and some accept credit cards. You can buy phonecards at KPN teleboutiques, post offices, station ticket counters and many newsagents. To call the international operator dial 0800 0410.

International Dialling Codes

From Amsterdam to:

UK:	00 44
Germany:	00 49
USA:	00 1
Spain:	00 34

POST

Post offices
Most PTT post offices (*postkaantoren*) are open Mon–Fri 9–5. Hoofdpostkantoor (head post office): ✉ Singel 250–256 ☎ 330 0555 ⊙ Mon–Wed & Fri 9–6, Thu 9–8, Sat 9–1.

TIPS/GRATUITIES

Yes ✓ No ✗		
Hotels (service included)	✓	change
Restaurants (service included)	✓	change
Cafés (service included)	✓	change
Taxis (service included)	✓	10%
Tour guides	✓	€1/€5
Porters (charge)	✓	change
Chambermaids	✓	€3/€5
Usherettes	✗	
Hairdressers	✓	change
Cloakroom attendants	✗	
Toilets (charge)	✗	

PHOTOGRAPHY

Light: although Amsterdam can be hazy, North Sea breezes usually sweep this haze away. After a summer shower the air has a sparkling, luminous quality.
Where you can photograph: some museums and other attractions do not allow you to take photographs; some forbid you to use flash; for some you need permission before you can use a tripod-mounted camera.
Where to buy film: film and camera batteries are readily available from photographic and tourist shops. Slides are called dias.

HEALTH

 Insurance EU nationals can obtain free medical treatment in the Netherlands with the relevant documentation (Form E111 for British citizens), although 10 per cent of prescribed medicine must be paid for. Private medical insurance is still advised and is essential for all other visitors. US visitors should check their insurance coverage.

 Dental Services For urgent, out-of-hours dental treatment, contact the Central Medical Service (☎ 592 3434).

 Weather Even at the height of summer, temperatures in Amsterdam rarely get much above 25°C and are usually cooler. If you plan to do a lot of sightseeing on foot at this time, wear sunscreen and drink plenty of fluids – carry a bottle of mineral water rather than stopping at pavement terraces for beers. Rain is possible at all times, and winter temperatures occasionally drop low enough to freeze the canals.

 Drugs Prescription and non-prescription drugs and other medical products are sold in *apotheeken* (pharmacies), recognised by a green cross sign. The addresses of nearby out-of-hours pharmacies are posted on pharmacy doors or windows. Despite their name, *drogerijen* (drug stores) do not sell medicines, but toilet articles and cosmetics.

 Safe Water Tap water is safe to drink all over the Netherlands. Bottled mineral water, often called by the generic name 'spa', after a popular Belgian label, is readily available in shops, restaurants and cafés.

CONCESSIONS

General
A 1-, 2-, or 3- day Amsterdam Pass, available from NBT and VVV offices, allows free admission to more than 20 museums and attractions, as well as other free and discount offers, and free use of public transport.

Students/youths
An inexpensive Cultureel Jongeren Pas (Cultural Youth Pass), available from VVV offices or Uit Buro and valid for a year, entitles anyone under 26 to free admission to many museums, as well as to discounts on cultural performances and events.

Senior Citizens
Many museums, attractions and performance venues have reduced admission prices for seniors.

CLOTHING SIZES

Netherlands	UK	Rest of Europe	USA	
46	36	46	36	
48	38	48	38	
50	40	50	40	Suits
52	42	52	42	
54	44	54	44	
56	46	56	46	
41	7	41	8	
42	7.5	42	8.5	
43	8.5	43	9.5	
44	9.5	44	10.5	Shoes
45	10.5	45	11.5	
46	11	46	12	
37	14.5	37	14.5	
38	15	38	15	
39/40	15.5	39/40	15.5	Shirts
41	16	41	16	
42	16.5	42	16.5	
43	17	43	17	
34	8	34	6	
36	10	36	8	
38	12	38	10	Dresses
40	14	40	12	
42	16	42	14	
44	18	44	16	
38	4.5	38	6	
38	5	38	6.5	
39	5.5	39	7	Shoes
39	6	39	7.5	
40	6.5	40	8	
41	7	41	8.5	

WHEN DEPARTING

- Contact the airport or airline on the day prior to leaving to ensure your flight details are unchanged.
- You are advised to arrive at the airport two hours before your flight is due to take off.
- Before departure, check the duty-free limits of the country you are entering.

LANGUAGE

Most Dutch people speak at least some English and many are fluent. This can make it frustrating if you want to practise speaking Dutch, as often a question you ask in Dutch will be answered in English. Not everybody speaks English, though, making it useful to know some Dutch words, and attempts to use them will be appreciated. The 'oo' (pronounced 'oa' as in load) and 'ee' constructions (pronounced 'ay' as in day) are particularly problematic for English-speakers and lead to common errors; as an example, remember the department store Vroom & Dreesman is pronounced 'Vrome & Drayssman'. If you pronounce 'ij' like English 'eye' you'll be close enough: for example *prijs* 'price'; *ontbijt* 'ontbite'.

hotel	*hotel*	breakfast	*ontbijt*
room	*kamer*	toilet	*toilet/WC*
single/	*eenpersoonskamer/*	bathroom	*badkamer*
double	*tweepersoonskamer*	shower	*douche*
one/two nights	*een/twee nachten*	balcony	*balkon*
per person/	*per persoon/*	key	*sleutel*
per room	*per kamer*	room service	*room service*
reservation	*reservering*	chambermaid	*kamermeisje*
rate	*prijs*		

bank	*bank*	American dollar	*Amerikaanse dollar*
exchange office	*wisselkantoor*	banknote	*papiergeld*
post office	*postkantoor*	coin	*wisselgeld/kleingeld*
cashier	*kassa*	credit card	*creditcard*
foreign exchange	*buitenlands geld*	traveller's cheque	*reischeque*
currency	*valuta*	exchange rate	*wisselkoers*
British pound	*Engels/Britse pond*	commission charge	*commissie*

restaurant	*restaurant*	dinner	*diner/avondeten*
café	*café*	starter	*voorgerecht*
table	*tafel*	main course	*hoofdgerecht*
menu	*menukaart*	dish of the day	*dagschotel*
set menu	*menu*	dessert	*nagerecht*
wine list	*wijnkaart*	drink	*drank/drankje*
lunch	*lunch/middageten*	waiter	*ober*

aeroplane	*vliegtuig*	single/return	*enkele reis/retour*
airport	*luchthaven*	first/	*eerste klas/*
train	*trein*	second class	*tweede klas*
station	*station*	ticket office	*boekingskantoor*
bus	*bus*	timetable	*dienstregeling*
station	*busstation*	seat	*plaats*
ferry	*veerboot*	non-smoking	*niet roken*
port	*haven*	reserved	*gereserveerd*
ticket	*reisekaart*	taxi!	*taxi!*

yes	*ja*	sorry	*excuseer/pardon*
no	*nee*	help!	*help!*
please	*alstublieft*	today	*vandaag*
thank you	*dank u wel*	tomorrow	*morgen*
hello	*dag/hallo*	yesterday	*gisteren*
goodbye	*dag/tot ziens*	how much?	*hoeveel?*
goodnight	*welterusten*	expensive	*duur*

INDEX

INDEX

Acknowledgements

The Automobile Association wishes to thank the following photographers and libraries for their assistance in the preparation of this book.

Amsterdam historical museum 16, BRIDGEMAN ART LIBRARY 23b The Nightwatch, c.1642 (oil on canvas) by Rembrandt Harmensz. van Rijn (1606-69), Rijksmuseum, Amsterdam, Holland, 24b Van Gogh's Bedroom at Arles, 1888 (oil on canvas) by Vincent van Gogh (1853-90), Rijksmuseum Vincent Van Gogh, Amsterdam, The Netherlands; MARY EVANS PICTURE LIBRARY 10b, 11a, 11b; HULTON GETTY 14b; GEORGE MCDONALD 46; PICTURES 80, 87, 89; EDDY POSTHUMA DE BOER 85, 90; SPECTRUM COLOUR LIBRARY 27b, 76, 78, 79, 82, 83; THEATRE INSTITUUT NEDERLAND 72b; WORLD PICTURES 81, 84, 88a, 88b; www.euro.ecb.int 119 (euro notes).

The remaining photographs are held in the Association's own library (AA PHOTO LIBRARY) and were taken by Ken Paterson with the exception of the following: Max Jourdan F/cover (b) tulips, (e) the Dam, (g) windmill, (h) woman on bike, (i) NEMO, (j) Rembrandt Museum sign, bottom, tulips; Alex Kouprianoff F/cover (d) gabled houses, 2, 5b, 13c, 15a, 16a, 17a, 18a, 19a, 20a, 21a, 22a, 23a, 24a, 25a, 26a, 32, 35, 36c, 43, 45, 50/51, 52b, 53b, 55b, 61b, 62b, 66b, 67b, 74/75, 91b, 122 a, 122b, 122c; Wyn Voysey front cover (a) cheeses, 6a, 7a, 8a, 9a, 10a, 12a, 13a, 14a, 28, 29, 31, 34a, 36a, 38, 39a, 40, 41, 42a, 44a, 48a, 51a, 52a, 55a, 56a, 59a, 60a, 61a, 62a, 64a, 65a, 66a, 67a, 68a, 70a, 72a, 75a, 77, 91a, 92, 93, 94, 95, 96, 97, 98, 99, 100, 101, 102, 103, 104, 105, 106, 107, 108, 109, 110, 111, 112, 113, 114, 115, 116,

Revision Management: Apostrophe S Ltd   Page layout: Barfoot Design

Dear Essential Traveller

Your comments, opinions and recommendations are very important to us. So please help us to improve our travel guides by taking a few minutes to complete this simple questionnaire.

You do not need a stamp (unless posted outside the UK). If you do not want to cut this page from your guide, then photocopy it or write your answers on a plain sheet of paper.

Send to: **The Editor, AA World Travel Guides, FREEPOST SCE 4598, Basingstoke RG21 4GY.**

Your recommendations…

We always encourage readers' recommendations for restaurants, nightlife or shopping – if your recommendation is used in the next edition of the guide, we will send you a *FREE* AA *Essential* **Guide** of your choice. Please state below the establishment name, location and your reasons for recommending it.

_____
_____
_____
_____

Please send me **AA *Essential*** _____

About this guide…

Which title did you buy?
  AA *Essential* _____
Where did you buy it? _____
When? m m / y y

Why did you choose an AA *Essential* Guide? _____
_____
_____
_____
_____

Did this guide meet your expectations?
  Exceeded ☐   Met all ☐   Met most ☐   Fell below ☐
  Please give your reasons_____
_____
_____
_____

continued on next page…

Were there any aspects of this guide that you particularly liked? _____

_____

_____

Is there anything we could have done better? _____

_____

_____

About you...

Name (*Mr/Mrs/Ms*) _____

Address _____

_____

_____ Postcode _____

Daytime tel nos _____

Please only give us your mobile phone number if you wish to hear from us
about other products and services from the AA and partners by text or mms.

Which age group are you in?
Under 25 ☐ 25–34 ☐ 35–44 ☐ 45–54 ☐ 55–64 ☐ 65+ ☐

How many trips do you make a year?
Less than one ☐ One ☐ Two ☐ Three or more ☐

Are you an AA member? Yes ☐ No ☐

About your trip...

When did you book? m m / y y   When did you travel? m m / y y
How long did you stay? _____
Was it for business or leisure? _____
Did you buy any other travel guides for your trip?
    If yes, which ones? _____

Thank you for taking the time to complete this questionnaire. Please send it to us as soon as
possible, and remember, you do not need a stamp (*unless posted outside the UK*).

Happy Holidays!

The information we hold about you will be used to provide the products and services requested
and for identification, account administration, analysis, and fraud/loss prevention purposes. More
details about how that information is used is in our privacy statement, which you'll find under the
heading "Personal Information" in our terms and conditions and on our website: www.theAA.com.
Copies are also available from us by post, by contacting the Data Protection Manager at AA,
Southwood East, Apollo Rise, Farnborough, Hampshire GU14 0JW.

We may want to contact you about other products and services provided by us, or our partners (by
mail, telephone) but please tick the box if you DO NOT wish to hear about such products and
services from us by mail or telephone. ☐

The Atlas

Acknowledgements
All pictures are from AA World Travel Library with contributions from the following photographers:
Max Jourdan: bulb fields at Keukenhof Gardens, window displays in Amsterdam, Amsterdam café
Alex Kouprianoff: Dam Square, Amsterdam
Ken Paterson: bicycle by canal

Day One

Day Two

Day Three

Day Four

Day Five

Day Six

Day Seven

www.theAA.com
The Automobile Association's website offers comprehensive and up-to-the-minute information covering AA-approved hotels, guest houses and B&Bs, restaurants and pubs in the UK; airport parking, insurance, European breakdown cover, European motoring advice, a ferry planner, European route planner, overseas fuel prices, a bookshop and much more.

www.aaa.com
AAA's website offers comprehensive information covering AAA-approved hotels and restaurants in the US. In addition, AAA can assist US citizens with obtaining a passport, reservations and tickets for cruise, tour, motorcoach, rail and air travel. AAA provides information on independent or escorted tours for individuals or groups and offers benefits on cruises, tours and travel packages.

The Foreign and Commonwealth Office Country advice, traveller's tips, before you go information, checklists and more.
www.fco.gov.uk

The official site of the Netherlands Board of Tourism, with a multitude of language options, has plenty of useful information.
www.visitholland.com

The website of the Amsterdam Tourist Board is a comprehensive source of information and advice on hotels, restaurants, museums, nightlife and more.
www.visitamsterdam.nl

GENERAL
UK Passport Service
www.ukpa.gov.uk

Health Advice for Travellers
www.doh.gov.uk/traveladvice

US passport information
www.travel.state.gov

BBC – Holiday
www.bbc.co.uk/holiday

The Full Universal Currency Converter
www.xe.com/ucc/full.shtml

Flying with Kids
www.flyingwithkids.com

A comprehensive site that covers the hot restaurants, clubs, nightspots, hotels and more. Reviews and generally up-to-date information.
www.amsterdamhotspots.nl

A virtual tour of Amsterdam (and other international cities) with viewer comments on attractions, restaurants, smoking coffee shops, and more.
www.channels.nl

TRAVEL
Flights and Information
www.cheapflights.co.uk
www.thisistravel.co.uk
www.ba.com
www.worldairportguide.com

The public transport network of trams, buses, metro trains and ferry boats in Amsterdam is comprehensive, but complex. Visit here for information on routes and tickets.
www.gvb.nl

Motorway Autobahn		Autosnelweg Autoroute
Road with four lanes Vierspurige Straße		Weg met vier rijstroken Route à quatre voies
Thoroughfare Durchgangsverkehr		Weg voor dorgaand verkeer Route de transit
Main road Hauptstraße		Hoofdweg Route principale
Other roads Sonstige Straßen		Overige wegen Autres routes
Parking place - Information Parkplatzrk - Information	P i	Parkeerplaats - Informatie Parking - Information
One way street Einbahnstraße		Straat met eenrichtingsverkeer Rue à sens unique
Pedestrian zone Fußgängerzone		Voetgangerszone Zone piétonne
Main railway with station Hauptbahn mit Bahnhof		Belangrijke spoorweg met station Chemin de fer principal avec gare
Other railway Sonstige Bahn		Overige spoorweg Autres ligne
Subway U-Bahn	M ·······	Ondergrondse spoorweg Métro
Tramway - Bus line Straßenbahn - Buslinie	● —— ●	Tram - Buslijn Tramway - Ligne d'autobus
Car ferry - Passenger ferry Autofähre - Personenfähre	– – – – ·······	Autoveer - Veerpont Bac pour automobiles - Bac pour piétonnes
Landing stage - Lock Anlegestelle - Schleuse	⊥ ⊏	Aanlegplaats - Sluis Embarcadère - Écluse
Church of interest - Church Sehenswerte Kirche - Kirche	✚ ✚	Bezienswaardige kerk - Kerk Église remarquable - Église
Synagogue - Mosque Synagoge - Moschee	✡ ☾	Synagoge - Moskee Synagogue - Mosquée
Monument - Police station Denkmal - Polizeistation	⌐ ●	Monument - Politiebureau Monument - Poste de police
Post office Postamt	✆	Postkantoor Bureau de poste
Hospital - Youth hostel Krankenhaus - Jugendherberge	✛ ▲	Ziekenhuis - Jeugdherberg Hôpital - Auberge de jeunesse
Airport bus - Camping site - Windmill Flughafenbus - Campingplatz - Windmühle	B △ ⅄	Vliegveldbus - Kampeerterrein - Windmolen Bus d'aéroport - Terrain de camping - Moulin à vent
Built-up area - Public building Bebaute Fläche - Öffentliches Gebäude		Bebouwing - Openbaar gebouw Zone bâtie - Bâtiment public
Industrial area - Park, forest Industriegelände - Park, Wald		Industrieterrein - Park, bos Zone industrielle - Parc, bois
Municipal boundary Stadtgrenze		Stadsgrens Limite municipale

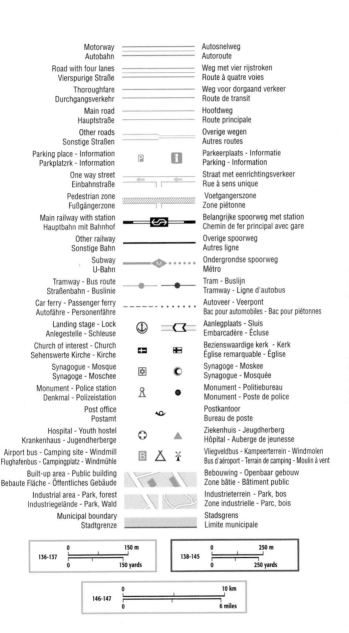

	0 150 m
136-137	0 150 yards

	0 250 m
138-145	0 250 yards

	0 10 km
146-147	0 6 miles

Maps © Mairs Geographischer Verlag / Falk Verlag, 73751 Ostfildern

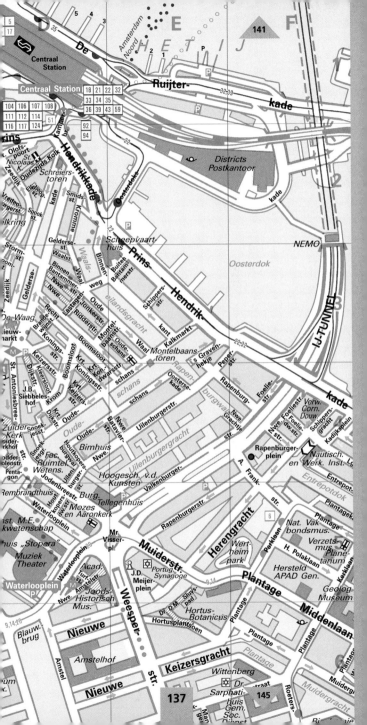

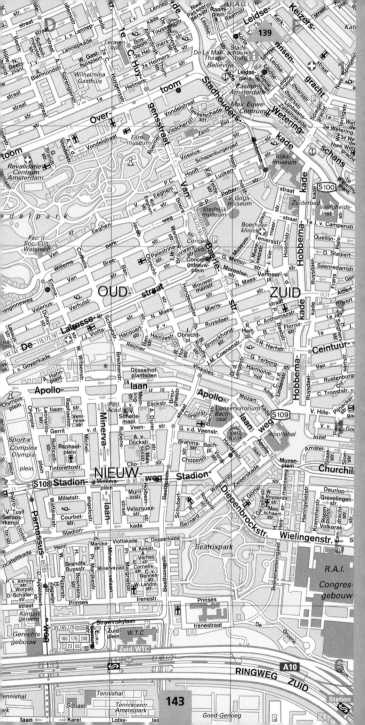

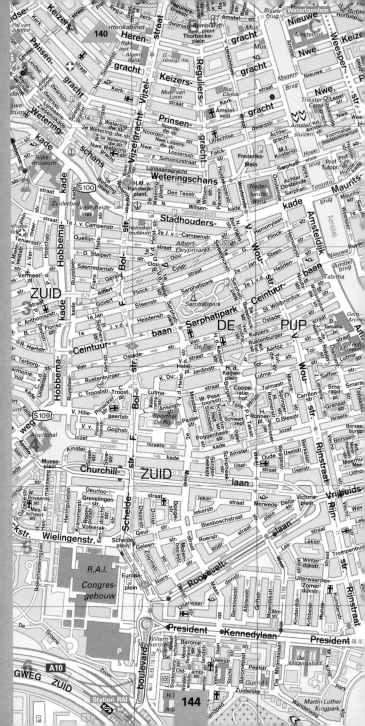

146

STREET INDEX